DETOUR
CENTRAL FLORIDA

DETOUR CENTRAL FLORIDA

HISTORY BY THE ROADSIDE

JENNIFER HUSMANN

Published by The History Press
An imprint of Arcadia Publishing
Charleston, SC
www.historypress.com

First published 2026

Manufactured in the United States

ISBN 9781467170390

Library of Congress Control Number: 2025944887

Notice: The information in this book is true and complete to the best of our knowledge. It is offered without guarantee on the part of the author or The History Press. The author and The History Press disclaim all liability in connection with the use of this book.

For Fr. Chris Hathaway, FSSP,
who encouraged me to learn about my home.

CONTENTS

TAMPA METRO AREA

SOUTHWEST CENTRAL (BRADENTON TO CHARLOTTE HARBOR)

CENTRAL LAKES REGION

TREASURE COAST

ACKNOWLEDGEMENTS

I would like to thank my parents for supporting my research and for lovingly accompanying me on my trips for this book. No one could ask for parents more encouraging—or more forgiving—than mine. I also want to thank my dear friend Suzan Sammons for her wisdom and guidance, without which this project couldn't have happened.

I will be forever thankful to The History Press and Chad Rhoad for seeing something in my stories.

I want to thank my husband, Ryan, for his encouragement of my dreams and for his unfailing patience with me.

I owe a debt of gratitude to my great-great-great-grandparents, those pioneering early Floridians, for paving the way for my children and me in that challenging and unforgiving Central Florida terrain. By their lives, they taught me there is something to love, and something to learn, in the shadow of the ancient oaks.

Above all, I want to thank the Lord Jesus, for gifting me with eyes to see the little journeys—and a heart to love them.

INTRODUCTION

Driving south down I-275 to Hyde Park to see extended family from my home in Lutz, I recall looking at the Sulphur Springs Water Tower—right at the halfway point—and imagining its origin. Sometimes I imagined a princess locked up beyond its ramparts, probably being held by a witch. Or I would envision myself at the top of the tower—maybe I was a pigeon—and I could see desert islands all the way across the gulf to Mexico from its pinnacle. Sometimes I just enjoyed its familiarity: it was always there, on the right side of the car when heading south, waiting for me among the clouds, a gentle river dotted with palm trees, coiling mysteriously at its base.

Later I learned that river that wound around my tower was the same river I crossed when I went to Lettuce Lake Park in Temple Terrace with my dad and again at the handsome castle downtown with the silver minaret toppers on its towers, where Granddaddy went to school (University of Tampa). *That is the same river? All the way from the park to the castle!* I recall marveling at this discovery. I began to realize my city was interconnected, in stories, in rivers, in people, in destinies.

Next, it came to light that a pirate had sailed up that same river past my tower and past my grandmother's apartment (a few hundred years before she moved in) and stolen cattle from some cattlemen who ranged beef before there was, well, anything at all in North Tampa. Later, a missionary paddled up its dark bends and named my grandma's neighborhood Terese (as in St. Terese), which morphed into *terrace*, eventually becoming what I knew as Temple Terrace.

By this time, I was no longer a child, but I retained a fascination with the ordinary stories behind everyday places. I read of a world of ancient history an ocean away, with timeline points much earlier than 1800. (1800 is *very* early for non-Indigenous Florida history.) The stories of the things I see right off my own road—the sandy little byway behind the cluster of orange trees next to the little white church or the route recorded on an old Spanish map of a coastal town I know well, before any hotels were built, before any people lived there—these are little journeys I crave.

This book is one of little journeys to splendid beaches, remote lighthouses, crumbling forts, former pirate stomping grounds, forgotten ghost towns, and secret gardens. I have included historical references and endnotes; after all, *true* stories matter (the Sulphur Springs Tower held a water reservoir—not a princess). All places herein lie within my native Central Florida, and each map point offers a unique snapshot of a locale as it stands today, asking these questions:

What am I looking at?
How did this get here?
Who lived here before, and why did they come?

It is my pleasure to share these little journeys with you.

WEST-CENTRAL

1

TO CEDAR KEY AND BACK

Head east on FL-24 until you reach the Gulf of Mexico in Florida's Big Bend, and you'll find yourself in the charming fishing village of Cedar Key. Fishing piers and stilt houses, pastel bungalows and folksy galleries, oyster beds and fish camps: Cedar Key defines Old Florida, and many of those who pass through end up never leaving.

Referring to a group of islands, the Cedar Keys are named for the abundant red cedarwood found in the area north of the Withlacoochee River and south of the Suwannee River. The main island today known as Cedar Key was formerly known as Depot Key because it was the southern terminus of the Florida Railroad, which connected the east and west coasts of Florida from Fernandina to the Gulf of Mexico. David Levy Yulee's choice of Cedar Key for the end of his rail line reveals the early importance of this area to Florida commerce. But Henry B. Plant, Florida's true railway magnate, chose Tampa rather than Cedar Key for his 1884 Plant Railroad, diverting traffic, commerce, and population ninety miles south. The name Depot Key fell into disuse with the departure of the final train in the 1930s, and the island itself became known as Way Key. The developed area of the cluster of islands, including present-day Way Key, is today known as the City of Cedar Key.

Cedar Key Light

Erected in 1854, the Cedar Key Lighthouse is the oldest lighthouse on the west coast of Florida. The tower crowns a sandy hill three miles from Way Key on Seahorse Key, named so for its shape. Early in Florida's history, dissident William Augustus Bowles formed an alliance with Creek and Seminole tribespeople and Black Seminoles, taking several Native wives and designating himself the director general of the "State of Muskogee." Bowles envisioned a militant and self-sufficient nation of Seminoles, Creeks, and escaped African slaves headed by him, totally independent from Spain, England, and the nascent United States. His primary activity occurred north of Cedar Key near Apalachicola, but his followers built a watchtower on Seahorse Key, Cedar Key's outermost island. Spanish forces destroyed Bowles's outpost in 1802.

Being the old stomping grounds of a self-styled "king" of a tiny nation seems colorful enough, but Seahorse Key's irregularities don't end there. Pirate Pierre LeBlanc kept guard of a cache of gold here around 1800, riding the length of the one-mile island on his trusty palomino, canvassing for possible intruders. His associate pirate Jean Lafitte had gifted him the

The ghosts of a bygone era permeate the landscape on Cedar Key, in the form of ramshackle fish huts and tumble-down docks among oyster beds and mangroves. *Author photo.*

horse and planned to return from New Orleans shortly, charging LeBlanc with guarding the loot. A snakeskin trader disembarked one evening to find LeBlanc and his palomino the island's sole occupants, and after some requisite peacocking, the men began to share stories and bond over a bottle of rum. LeBlanc apparently imbibed more than his strange guest and, later, thoroughly intoxicated, left to make his usual rounds on his palomino. After LeBlanc collapsed in a stupor at the site of the treasure, the snake dealer stumbled upon him. A brief tussle ensued, ending with the newcomer decapitating LeBlanc with his own cutlass and making off with the booty, leaving the horse pacing the shore. Locals say that a midnight visitor to Seahorse Key might catch sight of the pirate's faithful palomino, still patrolling the shoreline, guarding the crime scene, and looking for his ill-fated master.

When Florida became an American territory in 1821, federal agents used Seahorse as a short-term jail for Seminole Indians prior to their deportation to Arkansas and Oklahoma. After the island's use as a detention center, the federal government retained the archipelago due to its strategic location in the Gulf of Mexico.

Cedar Key became an important port after Florida achieved statehood, and a lighthouse was commissioned to assist mariners in entering the deepwater harbor. The current tower was built in 1852, a squat white beacon on a fifty-two-foot sandy hill, a relatively high elevation for the low-lying Cedar Keys. Confederate supporters extinguished the light at the start of the Civil War, but the Union eventually took the island, again making it a prison for Confederate troops. The light was restored after the war but abandoned in 1911 due to Cedar Key's fading prominence as a center of business and transport.

ATSENA OTIE KEY—FIRST SETTLEMENT

Atsena Otie, meaning literally "cedar key" in Seminole, is a tiny island a half mile off present-day Way Key and Cedar Key's first real settlement. Eberhard Faber, a German entrepreneur in the wood business, arrived at Atsena Otie in 1858 and began floating logs down the Suwannee River to his mill. At the height of the timber era, two mills operated from Atsena Otie, and a settlement of about fifty households thrived there for a short time.

In 1896, a massive hurricane demolished the timber mills on Atsena Otie, and the island never recovered. Most residents relocated to Depot Key or the mainland after the hurricane, and those who remained stayed only another generation. Today, the Andrews House is home to the Cedar Key Historical Society, a short walk from the Island Hotel, the oldest building in Cedar Key.

The last building on Atsena Otie was disassembled for scrap in the 1940s, and all that is left is an old cemetery, some building remnants, and a small pier. For twenty-first-century visitors, Atsena Otie is an interesting day trip accessible by boat; it is more or less an island ghost town.

ISLAND HOTEL

In 1859, Major John Parsons built the Island Hotel on Depot Key. The hotel now stands at 373 Second Street and is the oldest building in the city of Cedar Key. The ten-inch-thick oystershell walls have withstood dozens of tropical storms and hurricanes and by their nature expand and contract with the seasons. The fact that the building survived the Civil War indicates that the Union army likely used it as headquarters. After the war, it became a general store; rooms and meals began to be offered at some point prior to the devastating hurricane of 1896, which destroyed the timber mills. Naturalist John Muir's fabled journey from Indiana to the Gulf of Mexico culminated here in October 1886, and a weakened and malaria-ridden Muir visited the Island Hotel, at that time a general store. His journal, later published as *A Thousand-Mile Walk to the Gulf*, notes a handsome array of alligator and snakeskins, as well as a supply of quinine. Muir stayed in Cedar Key for a few months, recording botanical observations, before boarding a boat to Cuba and eventually California, where he assisted in founding the first Sierra Club.

The departure of the logging era ushered in a period of stagnation that lasted until after the Second World War. The Island Hotel remained open, but a series of shifty owners cast a shadowy gloom on the property, and at one point, rumors flew that it was being used as a house of ill repute. Another time, a mysterious fire was said to be the result of arson, set to collect insurance money. The final train departed the Cedar Key station in 1932, and the bridge connecting the mainland was broken by the constant battering of hurricanes. Few folks came or went, and the Island Hotel and the town reached a low point of neglect, disrepair, and depression. Remnants of the railway trestle connecting Way Key and the mainland still mark the site of the original railway bridge through the salt marshes and oyster beds.

Turtle Trail Art Gallery is one of many in and around the formerly remote fishing village of Cedar Key, off Florida's lonely leg. *Author photo.*

All of that changed when plucky, resilient "Gibby" Gibbs arrived in 1949 with his wife, Bessie. With good old-fashioned elbow grease and that steadfast will to find a way characteristic of so many early Florida settlers, Gibby and Bessie brought new life to the hotel and revitalized the entire town. Soon guests began to arrive, including artists, politicians, and celebrities. Jimmy Buffet enjoyed stopping into the Island Hotel in the 1970s, and a more laid-back atmosphere settled over it and the entire island. Oyster fishermen, honeymooners, and professors and students from University of Florida arrived from the mainland, lending the area an eclectic, quirky vibe.

Pastel-painted fence posts, neat tiny houses, and old wooden piers and fishing docks in various states of disrepair flank the shoreline of Cedar Key today, interspersed among the oyster beds and the fish shacks. Often sketched as what Key West used to be, the archipelago's charm is unmistakable, and many of its eight hundred or so residents are visitors who never went home.

2

ROSEWOOD

A SORE STILL HEALING

About halfway to Cedar Key after the turnoff from Highway 19, the Rosewood, Florida historic marker sits on the south side of FL-24 amid thick wilderness.

At one time, the area just beyond the historic marker was a quiet settlement of about twenty Black families; a contemporary observer described it as several collections of small painted residences with tidy yards. The area was home to a one-room schoolhouse and a few white clapboard churches, as well as a business or two. Its charming name reflects the wild roses clustered about the pink-tinted southern red cedar native to the area and also the namesake of Cedar Key.

Today, casual passersby remark on the apparent lack of human activity in the area; indeed, the route from Otter Creek to Cedar Key is bereft of dwellings, businesses, or parks. The eerie nothingness of this stretch of FL-24 feels uncanny, even given the remoteness of Levy County.

In 1983, *St. Petersburg Times* journalist Gary Moore drove up to Cedar Key looking for fresh content for a piece on weekend getaways in Florida's remote Big Bend. An investigative journalist at heart, he immediately noticed something odd: Cedar Key's population appeared to be 99 percent Caucasian, though a circa 1900 census recorded a population at least one-third African American. After receiving a few shrugs and punts by local whites, Moore posed the question to an elderly Black woman, "Where are all the black folks?" She replied, to his astonishment, "I know you are asking me about Rosewood—but I won't talk."[1]

How did this peaceful hamlet vanish into the cedar forest like the mist rolling off the pastures at sunrise?

On January 1, 1923, a mob of white men massacred the community while searching for Sylvester "Man" Carrier, who was suspected of assaulting a white woman in nearby Sumner. A full week of bloodshed ended in the deaths of five African Americans at the hands of an enraged mob, as well as two Caucasians. The roving band terrorized the entire community, and those who survived the massacre were haunted for generations to come. All survivors fled the area, leaving homesteads and residences, many heading to Chiefland, Archer, or Williston. Most residences were burned by the mob the week after their Black occupants evacuated. Whites from Sumner moved away too, escaping the notoriety of the site. Total silence fell over the event, with the survivors reluctant to dredge up painful memories and a white community unwilling to address the shameful guilt of the area's past sin. Soon this stretch of FL-24, at that time the Florida Railroad, was abandoned.

Gary Moore's digging and questioning opened the door to action and response on the decades-old wound far from healed. In 1994, a small group of survivors, by that time in their late eighties, filed a claim with the state legislature, imploring it to break the silence, acknowledge the crime, and make some reparation to the victims' families. In 2004, this historic marker was erected to memorialize the 1923 crime, to honor the community that recovered, and to remind future generations of the depravity of which man is capable when he gives himself up to hatred of his fellow man.

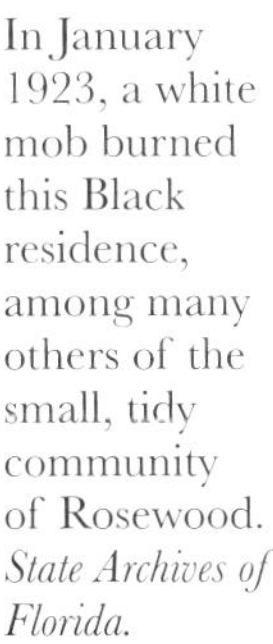

In January 1923, a white mob burned this Black residence, among many others of the small, tidy community of Rosewood. *State Archives of Florida.*

Beyond the Rosewood marker is a somewhat dilapidated three-story white Victorian home built in 1901. Known as the Wrights' place, it belonged to a white couple during the time of the Rosewood killings. The Wrights sheltered Black women and children during the week of horrors, hiding the innocents inside mattresses and in the rafters of the attic and even lowering little ones into the well, which still stands beyond the Rosewood Historical Marker on FL-24. They also helped Blacks evacuate Rosewood, hiding them until a train or cart became available and then assisting them under cover of night to safety.

The comparative elegance of the single Victorian home left in Rosewood and its role in mitigating the violence might just show the way to healing for the community. In 2020, the current owner, who had no idea of the area's history when she bought the land, gifted the home to the Real Rosewood Foundation. The foundation is now raising money to restore the old Wright place and to preserve it as a historical site, as a reminder of wrongs committed, and as a beacon of unity and friendship amid the area's deeply scarred past. Though the Wrights' place is on private property, beyond the structure are the remnants of the old Florida Railway, some iron spikes still visible, as well as the Rosewood Cemetery. Its decrepit and battered gravestones, many overgrown and illegible, are the sole reminder of the Rosewood era and the destroyed community and lives.

3

WHISTLESTOP ON FLORIDA RAILWAY

OTTER CREEK

College day-trippers from Gainesville use State Road 24 through Archer and Bronson and finally Otter Creek, the last signpost before the thirty-three-mile final stretch to popular fishing hamlet Cedar Key. Many pull over at Hershel's Quick Stop at the corner of US-19, owned and operated by an old-timer who has supposedly served passersby since the 1980s. After Otter Creek, FL-24 becomes a straight road flanked only by the cedar forests that gave Cedar Key its name, until it dead-ends at the Old Railroad Trestle bridge thirty-three long miles away. FL-24 traces the route of the Florida Railroad, completed right before the first shot was fired in the War Between the States.

Three hundred years prior to the Florida Railroad, Hernando de Soto crossed Otter Creek nearby here in 1539, and an 1853 map of Levy County identifies it as Otter Creek Ford, named for the abundance of otters along this tributary of the Waccasassa River.

The towns along FL-24 between Gainesville and Cedar Key were whistle-stops, and many residents descend from the railroad workers who laid the tracks for the first transpeninsular line. The line was disrupted by Union troops in the Civil War, and Henry B. Plant's railroad to Tampa (1884) quickly replaced the original Florida Railroad, rendering this area the remote forest and swampland it is today.

Levy County was named for David Levy, a Sephardic Jew from St. Thomas and the first Jewish U.S. senator, also named a "Great Floridian" in 2000. He supported the founding and growth of these tiny rural towns for

Named for the prolific river otter populating its waters, Otter Creek Ford was recorded on an 1853 map of La Florida, one of the earliest named waterways along Florida's remote Nature Coast. Hernando de Soto likely crossed this tributary of the Waccasassa River in 1539. *National Park Service.*

construction of his railroad, and the founders of Levy County chose him as their namesake.

One such founding family were the aptly named Strongs. Their homestead is just south of the FL-24 crossing of the Waccasassa, a Seminole word meaning "where the cattle are." Brothers Dan and Robert Strong arrived here in 1850, prior to Levy County's incorporation in 1852, and, like most old Otter Creek settlers, laid track for the Florida Railroad before they were pioneers. The railroad subcontractor awarded the brothers freedom upon completion of the work. The Strong brothers became founding fathers of Otter Creek and eventually opened a hotel, a store, and a large cattle ranch. The Strong family cattle brand is still on record at the county seat in Bronson.

Robert Strong joined the Confederate army in 1861, a passionate defender of his state's independence and what he knew as the Southern Cause. Later, Union forces captured and enslaved Strong and many other free men of color who joined the Confederate army, compelling them to join the enemy of the only home they knew. Indeed, Strong's gravestone memorializes him as a member of the Union infantry despite his clear Confederate allegiances.

His brother Dan Strong lived a long and prosperous life, dying at the age of 99. His wife, Joanna Strong, lived to be 107 and is said to have maintained a kitchen garden at the homestead until the final year of her long life. The ruins of Dan and Joanna's homestead and the Strong Family Cemetery lie in the woods south of FL-24 along the Waccasassa River. The Strongs' descendants donated portions of their ancestral homestead to Levy County for a school site in the 1970s.

Once a business hub of Levy County, a skeleton of downtown Otter Creek lies just past Hershel's, off FL-24 on the left heading west. The Strong Family Cemetery and old homestead ruins lie off an unmarked dirt road before the intersection of the FL-24 and US-19 deep in the forest along the slow-moving Waccasassa River. Visitors should exercise caution: the land is private property, and the locals here can be hostile to outsiders. Most of the Waccasassa River is accessible only by canoe, and a quiet paddle down this remote stretch is probably the most prudent way to experience the area.

The Rosewood massacre (1923) occurred just twelve miles west of this tiny ghost town, and the Strong family homestead, still owned by Robert and Dan's descendants, testifies to the resilience, ingenuity, and bravery of the earliest Floridians. They came to build the Florida Railroad, but their contribution reached beyond the final train.

4

THE YANKEETOWN GLASS HOUSE

Incorporated in 1923, Yankeetown[2] is a tiny hamlet of around five hundred, a sleepy settlement on the banks of the Withlacoochee River just before it flows into the Gulf of Mexico. It got its name one hundred years ago from a mail carrier who casually referred to it as "the Yankee town" for its then-predominantly Northern population. Picturesquely situated on a quiet stream overhung by ancient oaks, its small streets, tidy cottages, and neat churches testify to the New England sensibilities of its founders.

In 1919, one Aramis F. Knotts, a native of Indiana, built a home in this spot, which served as a fishing and hunting camp for his family and friends. Other Northerners followed, and the State of Florida incorporated the settlement as Yankeetown in 1923. The prettiest lane in Yankeetown is Riverside Drive, which runs parallel to Follow That Dream Parkway, Yankeetown's main artery.

In 1953, Knotts's nephew Eugene Knotts, a devotee of the Sarasota School of Architecture, designed a house that would allow him to sleep, eat, and live in the atmosphere of the shadowy and mysterious Withlacoochee River. Here on the shores of that very Withlacoochee River, a few miles from its mouth, is a house Eugene built entirely of glass.[3]

The Eugene-Knotts House was added to the National Register of Historic Places in 2018. The walls in the house are glass, excepting the roof and the two bathrooms. "The extensive use of glass in the exterior walls, the flat roof and the open floor plan aimed at blurring the lines between exterior and interior spaces are all character-defining features of the Sarasota School," reads its entry. The best vantage point for viewing the architectural novelty is accessed by paddling back up the Withlacoochee River and having put in downriver at the Yankeetown Boat Ramp.

The Sarasota School is a take on the highly utilitarian International style, which was prominent in Europe from 1920 to 1970. (The International style, in turn, arose from the more flamboyant and luxurious Art Deco style, which appeared in Paris in 1910 and is today associated with South Beach in Miami.) The Sarasota School keeps the simple lines and geometric shapes of Art Deco/International style but uses more glass, fine lines, and lightweight building materials to fit the sunny, relaxed climate of Central Florida. A seamless indoor-outdoor space, native landscaping, and a conscious absence of ornament are further qualities. Sarasota High School in Sarasota and the Warm Mineral Springs Motel in North Port are other examples of the Sarasota School, both occupying places on the National Register. The Sarasota City Hall and the Lido Shores community near St. Armands Key also espouse this muted, understated motif.

Beyond the Yankeetown Glass House is Bird Creek Bridge, the site of the 1962 Elvis film *Follow That Dream*, from which the road got its name.

The Eugene-Knotts House, also known as the Yankeetown Glass House, on the banks of the Withlacoochee River, was built in 1953. *National Park Service.*

Follow That Dream follows the members of a down-on-its-luck family who find themselves driving through Florida when they break down on the side of a remote road. Adventure with locals ensues, and the family ends up invoking homestead laws to keep the property. The film's director selected the eastern entrance of the Bird Creek Bridge for the site of the family homestead.

During filming, a local boy from Gainesville, a college town about an hour north of Yankeetown, accompanied his uncle to the set of *Follow That Dream*. The eleven-year-old met Elvis and, after returning home, promptly traded his best slingshot for an Elvis album. The encounter made a lasting impression: The young man was Tom Petty, one of North-Central Florida's most cherished sons.

In 1996, four Elvis Presley followers petitioned to change the name of Yankeetown's major road to commemorate the film. A statue of Elvis at the Inglis-Yankeetown Chamber of Commerce back toward US-19 commemorates Yankeetown's brief taste of fame.

5
DADE BATTLEFIELD
[1834]

Sumter County lies between Ocala and Tampa, formerly Fort King and Fort Brooke, respectively. In December 1835, Major Francis Dade marched 107 army troops from Fort Brooke to Fort King along a military route today known as the Fort King Trail. Chiefs Micanopy, Alligator, and Jumper had been shadowing the men for five days with their braves; they ambushed the troops, first killing Major Dade and then shooting down all other officers in rapid succession like fish in a barrel.[4] All but two of the American soldiers were killed, and one died of complications from his wounds five years later at the age of twenty-eight. This deadly clash was a major cause of the Second Seminole War (1835–42).

Today, the site of this brief but important battle scene is Dade Battlefield Historic State Park, which hosts an annual historical reenactment of the December 1834 tragedy each January. Just beyond the handsome iron archway and ticket kiosk is a trail leading off to the left into the hardwood forest. A series of white truncated obelisk monuments disappear into the trees. The first white obelisk in view marks the spot where Major Dade was killed, naturally at the head of the column of soldiers marching north (toward the park gate) that day. Seven other similar obelisks mark the locations of the other officers' deaths. These monuments are known as the *On This Spot* series of markers.

After the ambush, one of the two surviving soldiers, Ransom Clark, somehow struggled back to Fort Brooke in Tampa to report the attack. Seven weeks later, a well-armed detachment of soldiers marched from Fort

A series of truncated obelisks marks the precise locations of the first seven men to fall—beginning with Major Dade—at the devastating ambush of December 28, 1834. A total of 104 soldiers fell, including every officer in the column, leaving only two survivors. *Author photo.*

Brooke and found the entire scene untouched. The officers were buried to the east of the Fort King Trail, with the exception of Major Dade, who was laid to rest at St. Augustine National Cemetery. The enlisted deceased were accorded a proper burial to the west of the trail.

Beyond the *On This Spot* monument is a replica of the quick breastwork the soldiers erected during the brief reprieve when Chief Micanopy and his braves temporarily retreated. Having lost their commanding officers, the remaining soldiers speedily felled about twenty pine saplings and attempted to construct a makeshift fortification to protect themselves. They sadly reached only about a waist-high breastwork barrier before the Seminoles returned a few hours later and killed all remaining troops (save Ransom Clark and one other).

A path leads beyond the well-appointed visitors center to the Reenactment Mound and the Ancient Oak, an oak tree covered in resurrection fern, *Pleopeltis polypodioides*, a common plant species here in the rolling uplands north of Tampa. Found throughout the Southeast, resurrection fern's name is due to its curled, brittle, brown appearance during a dry spell and subsequent "resurrection" after a rainfall, which immediately restores the leaves to a lush, bright green. The Ancient Oak is several hundred years old, and it witnessed the battlefield prior to and during the massacre and all events since that dire day.

ABRAHAM'S TOWN

By 1800, escaped slaves from Georgia had fled to northern Florida and joined Seminole tribes, forming small pocket communities of Black Seminoles.[5] One such community emerged nearby what would later become Dade Battlefield. Catholic Spain did not permit the formal institution of slavery in its colonies, and therefore slavery was unlawful at that time in La Florida. The Black Seminole town was called Pilaklikaha, meaning "small ponds."

In 1826, an escaped slave named Abraham arrived in Pilaklikaha and joined the Black Seminole society that was thriving on this site. One source says there were about one hundred men, women, and children living here in thatch and daub homes, as well as some wooden dwellings. Well-tended fields of rice, melons, pumpkins, and green beans were also flourishing here.

Meanwhile, Seminole Chief Micanopy left the Alachua area after his uncle King Payne died and temporarily settled in this area. During this stay, Chief Micanopy met Old Abraham, whom he appointed his interpreter and ambassador to the English. An intelligent man who spoke perfect English, Abraham even accompanied Micanopy on a diplomatic trip to Washington, D.C. His service to the Indian chief resulted in Abraham's rise to prominence, and Pilaklikaha eventually came to be called Abraham's Town.

Although most of the inhabitants of Abraham's Town were not involved in the Dade Massacre, Chief Micanopy himself is said to have killed Major Dade. In retaliation, U.S. Army troops burned Abraham's Town, leaving nothing but ashes. Abraham had warned Micanopy that the soldiers were coming, and by the time they arrived, the entire town of Pilaklikaha had gone into hiding in Wahoo Swamp, about four miles west of Abraham's Town, visible today on the north side of County Road 476 near the intersection with Battlefield Parkway.

Later, Old Abraham was relocated to Oklahoma along with Chief Micanopy as part of the poorly conceived Indian Removal Act, which forcefully displaced Native Americans to designated reservations in modern-day Oklahoma and Arkansas. According to one source, Old Abraham became a Methodist minister in Indian Territory in Oklahoma; he died around 1870.

After Micanopy and Abraham's exile, a remnant of Black Seminoles partially rebuilt Pilaklikaha/Abraham's Town, though nothing remains of the settlement today. Today, Abraham's Town enjoys the distinction of having been the largest Black Seminole settlement in the state of Florida.

6

HOWEY-IN-THE-HILLS

Winding southwest through Lake County, US-19 traverses a chain of seven expansive blue lakes flanked by 1920s boom-era mansions, many of which are still standing. This cluster of lakes in the aptly named Lake County is interconnected by a network of charming canals. The Harris Chain of Lakes, named for the largest lake, Lake Harris, said to be even deeper than monstrous Lake Okeechobee in South Florida, connects to the St. Johns River and eventually to the Atlantic Ocean. Perhaps this connectivity with the Atlantic Seaboard explains why the Harris Chain of Lakes acquired a *Great Gatsby*–like scene during the Prohibition era. Businessmen from Illinois, Indiana, and Staten Island wintered here in Florida's Central Ridge. One such businessman was Raymond Robbins, who takes center stage at Chinsegut Hill. Another was William John Howey, founder of present-day Howey-in-the-Hills.

Howey-on-the-Hills is today a tiny incorporated town just over the Lake Harris bridge on its south side. In the early 1900s, the Illinois native purchased sixty thousand acres of land in what is today Lake County, for about $12 per acre. He cleared the land and planted orange trees, later reselling the land for $1,400 per acre. With this kind of business acumen, he soon grew wealthy enough to build a unique, Mediterranean-style mansion that still stands today. In 1925, Howey incorporated the area as Howey, Florida, serving as its mayor from 1925 to 1936. Shortly after incorporation, he changed the name to Howey-in-the-Hills to reflect the landscape. Howey liked to say Howey-in-the-Hills was the "Alps of Florida."[6]

The Howey Mansion was designed by then-rare female architect Katharine Cotheal Budd. Budd was born in 1860 and received no formal architectural training. Due to her unusual natural talent and extreme dedication to her craft, as well as informal learning at the elbow of Columbia University great William R. Ware, Budd was accorded an architectural license by the State of Georgia in 1920 at the age of sixty. She designed over one hundred homes during her lengthy career, including the Harry C. Duncan House, a Colonial Revival–style mansion also on the Harris Chain of Lakes.

Budd worked in the Mediterranean Revival style of architecture for Howey's estate, and she incorporated myriad intriguing details in the structure. The twenty-room rose stucco mansion's chief feature is the striking rear tower housing a curved stone staircase. The staircase features a sitting room situated halfway up, serviced by an additional hidden interior stairwell that leads to the first-floor butler's pantry.

A false wall in the foyer below the staircase opens to another smaller stairwell leading to a hidden room amounting to a sort of cellar. (True basements or cellars are almost unknown in Florida due to the state's high water table.) This is where Howey secreted his liquor cache during

A Prohibition-era cellar hides behind a false wall in the foyer of the Howey mansion in Lake County's small incorporated town of Howey-in-the-Hills. *David Bulit.*

The Howey mansion's interior spiral staircase encases a secret passageway leading to Mr. Howey's Prohibition-era liquor cache (visible to the right of the lower arch—false wall shown slightly ajar). Architect Katharine Cotheal Budd also added a charming sitting room just off the staircase, one of many intriguing details (visible through top arch). *David Bulit.*

Florida's Prohibition era. Florida's 1,350 miles of coastline made it a hotbed for bootleggers and rumrunners, and men of means like Howey took full advantage of the state's proximity to the Caribbean as well as its hundreds of miles of empty, pristine seashores. There is little doubt that Howey enjoyed regular deliveries of contraband liquor from the convenience of his own private dock.

In 1927, the Howey Mansion hosted a New York Civic Opera Company open-air concert that was attended by sixteen thousand people in four thousand automobiles. New York's well-heeled patrons of the arts mixed with Howey's Florida cracker neighbors, who were invited to join in the festivities as a thank-you from Howey for their generous hospitality in receiving a carpetbagger insurance salesman from New York.

The mansion declined after Howey's death in 1938 and was in a state of total disrepair by the end of the twentieth century. Brother businessmen and Florida natives Brad and Clay Cowherd often passed the crumbling mansion as children visiting their family's lake house in unincorporated nearby Yalaha, and as grown men and real estate developers they decided to restore the mansion to its former glory. They purchased the property in 2017 and meticulously restored the mansion to its original grandeur. At one time a vine-covered, quintessential "creepy old mansion" at the end of the street, the property now appears as it did in Florida's 1920s boom era.

Today, the Howey Mansion is open for historic tours, and a gardener's cottage and carriage house are available for rental on Airbnb. Even a stay in the actual mansion can be arranged for those able to pay upward of $6,000 nightly.

7

THE CHINSEGUT HILL STORY

Just off US-41, a few miles north of cute-as-a-button Brooksville is the Chinsegut Hill Historic Site, maintained by the Tampa Bay Historical Society and the U.S. Department of Agriculture. An account of Chinsegut Manor could fill an entire book with the bizarre saga of its owners, too lengthy for a collection of detour journeys off the highway. I will recount the events that bear most on our detour and leave it to the reader to investigate more, forming his or her own opinions about what transpired.

In 1842, a colonel from South Carolina acquired five thousand acres from the United States under the Armed Occupation Act, which provided for government grants of large tracts of Florida land to private citizens at no cost. In return, the new owners had to protect the land from incursion by Seminoles, build an inhabitable dwelling, and cultivate at least five acres for profit, within five years. Landowners were also required to provide militia service if necessary.

Of his five thousand acres, Colonel Pearson selected this hill for his homesite, as it was the most attractive plot in the tract. The original manor house was constructed of cypress timber hauled by oxcart from the mouth of the Weeki Wachee River in northern Tampa Bay. The vernacular wood frame was hand-hewn by a shipwright. Colonel Pearson used enslaved laborers to clear land and plant sugarcane, raise cattle, and cultivate citrus fruit, among other things; he named this spot Tiger Tail Hill.

He sold the property to the Edgertons, a pioneering family, who improved it over several years and then sold it to the Snow family. Both the Edgertons

Hernando County's picturesque Chinsegut Hill Estate was named for the Innuit word meaning "the spirit of lost things," an appropriate title considering the still-unsolved mystery of its owner's disappearance. *Author photo.*

and the Snows were laid to rest in the pioneer cemetery on site, visible under the oak tree to the west of the manor estate. The Snow family renamed the estate Snow Hill.

During the Snow Hill era, a child named Raymond Robins visited this site and resolved at the age of nine to one day own it. He was visiting from Staten Island, New York, but was staying with relatives in Brooksville because, tragically, his mother, a distinguished opera singer, had been committed to an insane asylum.

As a young man, Raymond went to law school but soon became disillusioned and unsatisfied with his profession. Next, he sailed to Alaska to prospect for gold, but somewhere in the darkness of the Klondike, he went missing. His older sister Elizabeth traveled to Alaska to find him. She wrote about these events in her novels *Magnetic North* and *Come and Find Me*. Elizabeth did find Raymond, very ill and weak, and she encouraged him to return to civilization.

In 1905, at the age of twenty-eight, Robins achieved his dream and acquired Snow Hill. At around the same time, he and his wife became heavily involved in progressive politics, eventually traveling to Russia. At first, Robins merely oversaw the Red Cross food distribution during the Bolshevik upheaval, but he eventually became involved with Lenin, who he at one point met with three times a week. His wife, back in the States by this time, planted an acorn at Chinsegut that Robins would name Lenin Oak after the Communist dictator. As you will see from the events that follow, no one knows which oak is Lenin Oak.

Back at the manor, the Robinses invested much in improving the property, adding four bathrooms, a second kitchen, a second fireplace, and a widow's walk (no longer extant) as well as a study, a library, and a music room. They hosted literary greats and others such as Thomas Edison and Marjorie Kinnan Rawlings, James Cash Penney of department store fame, William Jennings Bryan, and various Soviet dignitaries.

On Chinsegut Hill grow two ancient oaks, one named Altar Oak, to which Robins turned for prayer each morning on waking; a second is Ascension Oak. Altar Oak and Ascension Oak are down the hill descending east from the manor and are well marked. Robins had a ladder and a platform constructed in the upper boughs of aptly named Ascension Oak so he could be "closer to heaven." The treehouse-like platform is extant and can even be climbed by visitors.

An ancient oak draped in Spanish moss shelters a hillside pioneer graveyard a stone's throw from Chinsegut Manor. Raymond Robins, Chinsegut's final owner, is buried nearby, set apart from the other deceased. *Author photo.*

Raymond rechristened the property Chinsegut, Inuit for "the spirit of lost things."

In September 1932, Robins was wrapping up a tour of 286 cities in which he had spoken in favor of Prohibition, of which he was an ardent supporter. He was on his way to meet President Herbert Hoover, a personal friend, when he abruptly vanished from the streets of New York. Two separate acquaintances, one a friend of two decades, testified to seeing Robins in Chicago the day after his disappearance.

After a frantic national search, he was found two months later in Wittier, North Carolina, near Smoky Mountains National Park, where he had taken up a new identity as Reynolds Rogers. He was placed in an insane asylum in Asheville, North Carolina. Although his wife, Margaret, visited him there, it seemed to take three visits before he recognized her. He returned to Brooksville on Thanksgiving of that year and, after some rest, resumed life as he had known it prior to his September disappearance.

Although Robins was diagnosed with amnesia from exhaustion and overwork, the citizens of Wittier insisted he knew who he was the whole time. While in North Carolina, he subscribed to a Brooksville newspaper, having it sent to him there under his alias R. Rogers. Also, he abruptly left a stopover in Balsam, North Carolina, when he heard Floridians were arriving soon. Moreover, he spoke extensively of his time in Alaska and shared with locals that he knew Herbert Hoover and FDR (which he did). Even the similarity of his assumed name, Reynolds Rogers, to his legal name, Raymond Robins, would seem to suggest that he knew who he was all along. Whether amnesia really caused Robins to disappear remains a mystery to this day. For my part, I couldn't help but chuckle when I heard about this apparent bout with amnesia: It seems too perfect that such a fate would befall a man from "the spirit of lost things."

Two years later, Robins fell from a thirty-foot height while trimming a tree, which left him paralyzed for the rest of his life. Nonetheless, he lived another nineteen years. Both Robins and his wife are buried under an oak tree at Chinsegut Hill. They left the property to the federal government for research and experimental purposes.

One other bit of local history regarding the Lenin Oak question: In 1961, a troop of Boy Scouts were hiking up Chinsegut Hill and found a plaque memorializing the Lenin Oak as such. The Scout leader brought the plaque to the attention of the *Tampa Tribune*, which published it on the front page. National attention, fury, and "red-baiting" as the 1960s witch hunt for Communists is sometimes called, descended on Chinsegut Hill and the small, unassuming community of Brooksville, Florida. The USDA ordered the superintendent of the Chinsegut agricultural reservation to destroy the plaque, which he did by melting it down and throwing the remains into Lake Lindsey. The above account is more thoroughly described in the Chinsegut Manor's file with the National Register of Historic Places[7] archives and in the book *Reform and Recovery: The Life and Times of Raymond Robins*.

A walk toward the bench beyond the Edgerton Family Cemetery overlooks the gently sloping green valley below, where a few small farm buildings and cattle dot the hillsides. This vantage point offers a scenic overlook unique in Central Florida. Views like this caused one Brooksville real estate prospector in the 1920s to tout the area as being "the most un-Florida land imaginable!"[8]

The USDA still owns the land in this area from its bequest by the Robinses. The Tampa Bay Historical Society leads tours of the manor on weekends and maintains the estate.

8

HERNANDO COUNTY COURTHOUSE

THE CROWN JEWEL OF HERNANDO COUNTY

Hernando County was named after Spanish explorer Hernando de Soto and is the likely site of his 1539 crossing of the Withlacoochee River. The Spanish conquistador made landfall at Tampa Bay, near present-day De Soto National Monument in Bradenton. He and about six hundred men—knights, artisans, priests, scribes, boatwrights, and soldiers (not to mention several hundred pigs)—set out to explore the interior of the southeastern United States. De Soto and most of the men would die on this expedition as a result of clashes with Native Americans or disease.[9]

Although their trail is still being precisely mapped, historians agree that it likely followed present-day US-301 from Bradenton to Bushnell and then up US-41 from Bushnell to Tallahassee. The definitive study thus far on the 1539 route, commissioned by the National Park Service and completed in 1988, suggests that they crossed the Withlacoochee River, which traces the Hernando County boundary with Sumter.

US-41 bisects the Brooksville Historic District, enrolled on the National Register of Historic Places. Brooksville is the county seat and was named for South Carolina Democratic senator Preston Brooks, who is best known for having beaten abolitionist Charles Sumner on the floor of the U.S. Senate with a cane. (Brooks later testified that he meant no real harm and that he chose the implement specifically so as not to inflict a *fatal* injury!)[10] Sumner was badly injured and did not resume his Senate seat for two years. The Massachusetts legislature reelected Sumner while he was convalescing, allowing the seat to sit vacant during his absence reportedly as a reminder of Southern brutality. Brooks was administered a token criminal sentence; his constituents reelected him the following term. Both men became heroes of their respective regions following the incident.

As US-41 becomes East Jefferson in its brief jaunt through Brooksville, the May-Stringer House sits gracefully on the north side of the highway. Built in 1856 and expanded to its current size in 1880, the May-Stringer house is a four-story, seven-gable gingerbread-trim Victorian mansion. Marina May Saxon lived here with her husband, Frank, before she died giving birth to their daughter. The two-year-old daughter later died in the house; both are buried on site. Because of the home's sad history, the May-Stringer House is widely believed to be haunted. The Hernando County Historical Society offers free tours of the gingerbread Victorian daily.

Just south of the May-Stringer House lies the Saxon House (1875). When his wife, Marina, died, Frank married Talulah Hope, the daughter of one of the first families in Brooksville. He built this vernacular wood-frame home for Talulah, incorporating Queen Anne Victorian influences such as a steep roof, an asymmetrical design accomplished in this case by the southern quarter of the façade protruding out past the porch, lattice work on the trim and railings, and a broad front porch spanning the width of the façade. The Saxon House is now a privately-owned wedding and events venue.

At the corner of Main Street and US-41 sits the historic Hernando County Courthouse. Prior to its construction in 1913, several wooden courthouses located in the same spot were lost to fire. The red brick Neoclassical Revival structure, with white columns and latticed windows, was designed by South Carolina architect William Edwards, who also designed the Sumter County Courthouse and several buildings on the University of Florida campus. The courthouse is often called the crown jewel of Hernando County.

A few interesting events surrounding the courthouse and its predecessors have occurred since the county seat was moved to Brooksville from the coastal town of Bayport in 1856. The present structure was completed in the autumn of 1913, and shortly thereafter a cadre of mischievous youth disassembled a wooden buggy parked on the street nearby and reassembled it on the flat roof of the noble and venerable center of law and order. An amusing spectacle greeted the townsfolk on waking that morning after Halloween 1913.[11]

Back in 1885, prior to the construction of the current brick building, a shootout occurred on this spot involving three brothers. At that time, every male resident aged seventeen to fifty was required to dedicate six days of labor annually or pay a fee of fifty cents. The young trio asserted that they

The sober white columns and original red brick of the Hernando County Courthouse (1913), "the Crown Jewel of Hernando County," mark the center of Brooksville, a Deep South small town surrounded by hills and pastures. *Author photo.*

would do no such thing, and when the county sheriff arrived to collect the tax, he went away empty-handed. The fellows were subpoenaed to appear at the courthouse, and it was circulated about town that they would report as ordered but would do so fully armed.

A small crowd of sympathizers and detractors gathered around the courthouse steps to see the excitement, and the tension was palpable. The brothers remained belligerent, a riot ensued with supporters on each side, and all three brothers were mercilessly shot and killed in a barrage of gunfire. The fact that the young men were Black caused new animosities to arise between the Black and the white community here, and a general feeling of uneasiness settled over the town, not soon to be lifted.[12]

Also significant in the historic district is the Brooksville Train Depot. Along with a one-room schoolhouse, it is advertised as a "historic museum'" but with inconsistent, limited hours and frequent seasonal closures. More compelling is the shady greenspace with a small stream stretching westward toward Main Street from the tiny historic site. Behind the train depot is also The Good Neighbor Trail, a paved recreation trail tracing the 1885 branch line that connected downtown Brooksville to the Florida Southern Railway. It linked up at the town of Croom, now abandoned, but formerly a thriving junction serving several industries, most notably timber and turpentine. The Withlacoochee State Forest now envelops the Croom ghost town, but some crude structures remain, including the 1900 Thomas house, some remnants of the old railroad, and a few small family cemeteries.[13] Therefore, the ten-mile Good Neighbor Trail connects cyclists and runners to the Withlacoochee State Trail, as the Brooksville branch line once connected Brooksville railway passengers to the Florida Southern Railway.

In 1885, citizens of a tiny municipality like Brooksville fought long and hard for a railway connection to an industrial hub like Croom. In a reversal of fortunes, Brooksville is now a thriving county seat lined with charming teahouses and historic manors, and the once bustling town of Croom is all but lost in the sands of time.

A quaint streetscape sits just north of the train depot, as immense oak trees covered in Spanish moss hang low over the historic brick road. This stretch of South Brooksville Avenue, from Liberty Street to Early Street, is home to a number of historic residences, and the entire residential neighborhood is on the National Register of Historic Places. The Coogler-Claflin House (1913) at 133 South Brooksville Avenue is a handsome Greek Revival mansion with twelve smaller columns creating a verandah and four larger and more prominent columns supporting the triangular upper part of a portico in the Greco-Roman style. The Frazee House (1915) at 302 South Brooksville Avenue is a fine example of pure Queen Anne–style architecture with a steeply pitched metal roof and a three-story tower at its north side to create the asymmetry. A potpourri of other architectural styles influences the area, including Florida Cracker, bungalow, and Spanish Mission–style residences.

9

"CATHOLIC TOWN"

SAN ANTONIO AND ST. LEO ABBEY

Between the Bushnell and County Road 52 exits off Interstate 75 and paralleling the highway meanders a forty-minute scenic route through rolling hills and farmland, hidden in plain sight as it were. Few motorists find sufficient reason to investigate this rural backcountry, but the lucky few who do find themselves seemingly transported to Amish country in Pennsylvania or Ohio based on their surroundings. Though rather common in other states, Hernando County's green, hilly pastures, picturesque silos, red barns, and winding roads are unique in the Sunshine State.

Amid this meandering byway sits St. Leo University, founded in 1889, when San Antonio Catholic Colony's founder, Judge Edmund F. Dunne, donated his Lake Jovita home (not extant) to the Benedictine monks for a college and an abbey.[14] A real estate attorney at the time, he had assisted land developer Hamilton Disston of Pennsylvania in drafting transfer documents and deeds for the four million acres Disston had just purchased in Florida. (It's worth noting that this is one of the largest single private purchases of land in history.) Disston paid Dunne for the legal work in kind with 100,000 acres south of Brooksville, Florida.

Judge Dunne surveyed his newly acquired land and discovered Lake Jovita on his new property on February 15, St. Jovita's feast day on the Roman Catholic calendar. Dunne named Lake Jovita, the expansive, crystal-clear lake on which the abbey sits, for the Roman martyr who died in the year 120.

St. Leo University, St. Leo Hall, and Holy Cross Church are accessible by turning into the university's main entrance on Palm Boulevard. The university campus is walkable and beautiful; it is worth stopping to take a look. The sandstone Italian Romanesque Revival church rises picturesquely from the peaceful green of the college campus; the chalky limestone monastery, mined from the quarry in Brooksville and built by the monks themselves, stretches eastward toward St. Francis Hall, which houses the office of the sitting university president. Prior to the construction of the monastery, the brothers resided in the second story of a dormitory, in the midst of college students and campus activities—not ideal for the cloistered, contemplative life. The current St. Leo Hall was constructed by the monks between 1898 and 1912. The monastery faces the tranquil and picturesque Lake Jovita, a blue pool among gently rolling green hills.

Construction of the abbey church began during the Great Depression and took nearly two decades to complete. The buff sandstone of its masonry was mined in Meinhard, Indiana, a quarry used previously for an abbey there. A unique bartering arrangement existed between abbots: the St. Leo

"The Church That Orange Juice Built," Holy Cross Church at St. Leo Abbey in San Antonio, was constructed from pale yellow sandstone quarried near a monastery in Indiana. St. Leo traded the monastery-grown oranges for its building materials. A northbound truck loaded with citrus returned to Florida a week later carrying the cream-colored rock for the walls of the abbey church. *Author photo.*

monks sent monastery-grown oranges to Indiana, and on the return truck, St. Meinhard Abbey sent sandstone. In 1944, the *Orlando Sentinel* reported thirty-two truckloads of sandstone had so far arrived from Indiana; sixty-eight truckloads of citrus fruit had traveled north from San Antonio. For this reason, the abbey church is sometimes referred to as "the house that orange juice built."[15]

Ora et Labora ("Pray and work") is a key principle of the Rule of St. Benedict; it makes sense, then, that the labor of Benedictine monks is the backbone of much of San Antonio's infrastructure. In addition to constructing the buildings at the abbey and growing oranges for trade with the Indiana monastery, the monks here also cultivated sugar cane, melons, and strawberries. In 1890, the brothers constructed the train depot, now the only remaining depot of the Orange Beltway. In 1896, one Brother Leo was appointed mail carrier, boating across Lake Jovita to the train depot to deliver the mail daily.

Holy Cross Church keeps informal hours and is more or less open to visitors between morning and evening prayers, known as Lauds and Vespers in religious communities. Abbot Isaac Camacho offers Mass at 10:00 a.m. on Sundays and at noon on weekdays.

Constructed in 1890 by Benedictine monks, San Antonio's train depot is the only remaining train depot of the former Orange Belt Railway, which connected Sanford to St. Petersburg. *Author photo.*

From the intersection of Abbey Court and CR-52 extends a small unmarked stairway leading up the berm into the woods beyond. The trail leads to the Our Lady of Lourdes Grotto, hand-built in 1916 by Henry Moeller, a friend of Abbot Mohr, who described Moeller as "a roamer from Switzerland and a good builder in stone."[16] The abbot commissioned the grotto in thanksgiving for the favorable outcome of a lawsuit involving a property dispute over the forty-acre tract south of CR-52 on which the grotto sits. For decades thereafter, the sitting abbot led a procession of St. Leo students across the road and through the forest to offer Mass at the grotto on each Feast of the Immaculate Conception (December 8).

At his own request, Abbot Mohr was buried here at the grotto when he died in 1931. A later abbot erected a memorial to the college's fourteen students who died in World War II, as well as an additional monument commemorating the death of a St. Leo college student killed in the Korean War.

The university grounds, the monastery, the church, and the grotto are open to the public for quiet prayer and meditation.

TAMPA METRO AREA

10
GREEKTOWN
TARPON SPRINGS

Around 1873, a turtle fisherman from Key West got his nets tangled in a swath of shallows near Anclote Key, off the shore of what is now Tarpon Springs, where the Anclote River empties into the Gulf of Mexico. Sponging had become a lucrative business in Key West since British Bahamians discovered sea sponge colonies in 1820. The turtle fisherman forgot his tangled net when he discovered what it had snagged: massive beds of the rare, prized sea sponge.

Hundreds of square miles larger than the Key West beds, these virginal sponge colonies lay untouched at the bottom of the shallow water near the barrier islands of the west coast of Florida. The Conchs (a colloquial term for white Europeans who settled in Key West) began moving their operations in huge numbers to Tarpon Springs, and the American sponging trade flourished in the last few decades of the nineteenth century.

The Conchs gently drew the sea sponge from the shallows, embarking in teams of two or three per skiff, with one or two men paddling and another man using a long pole with a hook on its end. He stood in the rowboat, hook ready, scanning for sponges, and then speared the sponge from the bottom of the gulf and deposited it in the hull of the boat. To assist visually, the spongers used a device known as a glass-bottom bucket, which allowed them to see the sponges in the bottom of the gulf even in rough waters. Tarpon Springs residents, as well as Conchs, worked the sponge boats in this manner peacefully for several decades. The sponges were usually brought back to Key West and then shipped to New York, where they were sold for a generous profit throughout the United States.

New York native John Cheyney launched the first large-scale commercial sponging operation here in 1890. After several years of explosive success, he ran into another sponger in New York—a surprise, to say the least, since at that time the Florida Gulf Coast was one of only two locations in the world suitable to the growth of *Spongia officinalis*. A native of Greece, John Cocoris told Cheyney that his family had been sponging in the Dodecanese Islands of his homeland for centuries. (Diving for sea sponges had even been an Olympic sport in ancient Greece.) Cheyney immediately hired Cocoris and his Greek crew to move across the world and work for him in Tarpon Springs.

Cocoris, though, didn't mess around with small skiffs and hooks. Instead, his youthful Greek crewmen worked forty-foot sponging boats, donning heavy diving suits and fifty-pound iron boots to keep from floating to the surface. In this way, they collected sponges rapidly with their hands. This Greek diving method had been perfected by ancestral sponging traditions over centuries: the diving suits and heavy boots allowed them to reach the deepest, best sponges, which were not as accessible by way of the American hook method. The superior Greek diving technique rapidly overtook the American method.

The Conchs felt pushed out by the Greek spongers, who excluded the Americans from their crews, dismissing them as culturally and professionally inferior to the Greek expert spongers. Tension continued to brew between the Greeks and the Conchs over the next decade, finally climaxing in a series of raids and attacks, including several killings in 1915. Because Key West was the commercial headquarters of the sponging industry, much of the violence took place there. The so-called Sponge Wars were disorganized and loosely waged, but if there was a winner, it was the Greeks. By about 1920, the Conchs had surrendered the beds and moved away from their activities in Tarpon Springs, returning primarily to Key West.[17]

Meanwhile, more Greek families immigrated to the shores of the Anclote River. In addition to sponge boats and processing facilities, they built homes and churches according to their native traditions, and Tarpon Springs became an enclave of Greek culture. Today it boasts the highest concentration of ethnic Greeks in the United States.

Black spongers fared better than their white counterparts. Black Floridians fished many more decades with the Greek spongers, reaching a professional and social alliance that had been unattainable for the Conchs. Rose Cemetery is the oldest African American cemetery in Pinellas County, and it

Rare sponge beds off Tarpon Springs drew Greek spongers from the Dodecanese Islands in Greece, for whom generations of sponge diving had become a family business and a cultural identity. Sponge docks in Tarpon Springs off Dodecanese Boulevard. *Author photo.*

testifies to the settled presence of African Americans in Tarpon Springs and the community's respect and appreciation for their contributions.

Descendants of the original Greek spongers still harvest sponges along the Gulf Coast to this day, and thousands of sea sponges can still be seen in great heaps all along the docks at Dodecanese Boulevard.

ST. NICHOLAS GREEK ORTHODOX CATHEDRAL

East of and more inland than the Sponge Docks is St. Nicholas Greek Orthodox Cathedral. The congregation was founded in 1907 and took as its patron St. Nicholas, patron of Greece and of seafaring people. Constructed in 1943, the cathedral is an outstanding example of Byzantine architecture, replete with stunning iconography, more than sixty stained-glass windows, and a domed rotunda painted lavishly with figures of Christ and the saints. White marble dominates the space; it was quarried at Mount Penteli, near Athens, and was gifted to the congregation by the nation of Greece. An *iconostasis* (altar screen), in keeping with the Byzantine tradition, veils the holy space where the priest offers the divine liturgy. The cathedral is open to visitors daily.

Back in the courtyard stands a handsome bronze relief statue of a teenage boy holding a cross up to the dazzling blue sky, the dome of the cathedral looming auspiciously in the background. The sculpture is an ode to the annual Epiphany rite, which takes place just one block west of the cathedral in Spring Bayou.

Every January 6, after a lavish ceremony, the entire congregation proceeds to the bayou, and a young lady, known as the dove-bearer, releases a white dove symbolizing the Holy Spirit, a reference to the baptism of Christ in the Jordan. Then the bishop casts a weighted cross into the water, and the young men of the congregation dive for the cross. The lad who successfully retrieves the cross and presents it to the bishop receives a special blessing and is said to enjoy health and prosperity for the whole year.

This beloved ceremony occurs in Greece as well, but Florida's mild climate allows for a much larger and more elaborate dive each January 6. The diving for the cross invokes both the historical baptism of Christ, celebrated as part of the feast of the Epiphany, and also pays tribute to the ancestral sponging work that has so manifestly shaped this community. The ceremony is open to the public.

11

PHILIPPE PARK

A PIRATE REPENTS

Safety Harbor refers to both an inlet of Old Tampa Bay and a municipality on its northern coast. In the 1700s, pirates infested the coves of this area, and waterborne vessels were out of harm's way once they reached Safety Harbor.

Philippe Park spans the coastline of Safety Harbor, including its high point, a protuberance with an ancient Indian burial mound. In the early 1840s, this stretch of coastline was an isolated citrus plantation.

Not far from the point are two markers for its founder, Odet Philippe, one apparently a gravestone. Most traditional accounts[18] hold that Odet Philippe was born in Lyon, France, in 1789 to a noble family. (For this reason, he is sometimes known as Count Philippe.) A great inventor of tall tales, especially autobiographical ones, he claimed to have been a childhood friend of Napoleon Bonaparte and even to have been his personal surgeon. He named his boat *Rey* after one of Napoleon's ships, and his citrus groves were called St. Helena's, which was the rock island on which Napoleon was exiled. (Safety Harbor lies on a peninsula, not an island.)

Evidence shows that Philippe ended up in the Caribbean because he was captured by the British in the Battle of Trafalgar and promised to desert the nation of France in exchange for his release in the Bahamas. His colorful, adventurous early years also took him to Cuba, where he was instructed in the art of cigar-making, and Key West, where he became involved in the lucrative salvage business. Key West was fast becoming the richest city

Odet Philippe, Pinellas County's first permanent resident, shown here around 1820, was friends with Napoleon Bonaparte before he brought the grapefruit to Florida's citrus industry. *State Archives of Florida.*

per capita in the United States through the industry of wrecking, in which a crew strips shipwrecks of all valuable materials to be sold at auction or elsewhere. Impoverished Philippe, though noble by birth, assembled a huge cache of assets in Key West, likely in the business of salvaging.

Famed pirate and slave smuggler John Gomez captured and then befriended Philippe. Though no evidence exists that Philippe had medical training, he was widely acclaimed as a natural healer; Gomez spared his life at first only because of the valuable medical care Philippe provided to Gomez's crew. In Philippe's years on board the working pirate ship, Gomez often told him of a high point in a pleasant harbor at the northern reaches of what is now Tampa Bay.

Philippe later left the pirate life and spent time in Charleston, where he continued to amass a small fortune. He married Dorothee de Desmottes and had three daughters, bringing them to that high point in the pleasant harbor of which Gomez had spoken. The Philippe family homesteaded near the ancient Indian Tocobaga Temple Mound, which is visible to this day a stone's throw from Philippe's marker. As culturally insensitive as it may seem to the modern mind, Indian burial mounds in Central Florida proved ideal for nineteenth-century pioneer homesites due to their high-and-dry situation. Indeed, Philippe and his family survived the infamous 1848 hurricane that carved out John's Pass only by taking refuge on that very temple mound.

At St. Helena's, Philippe cultivated grapefruit trees, the first in Florida, and in 1963 was admitted posthumously to Florida Citrus Hall of Fame for his contributions. Grapefruit was reserved for the tables of the wealthy in Philippe's day but today comprise 20 percent of Florida's citrus crop production. He learned to grow the prized fruit in Cuba and brought his specialized knowledge to Florida. Many attribute the popularity of grapefruit in Florida today to Philippe's work.

Although Philippe is best known for his plantation in Safety Harbor, he spent about one hundred dollars on a few lots "in the town of Tampa," near Fort Brooke, no longer extant, and there established several businesses, including a pool hall and a cigar shop. From his experiences as the cigar maker's apprentice in Cuba, Philippe brought Cuban cigar making to Tampa, where the craft still flourishes in historic Ybor City.

Much ink has been spilled over the authenticity of the biography of this colorful character, and recent historical scholars believe he was actually the child of a French officer from Lyon and a local woman in the French province of Haiti. In fact, the Odet Philippe historic marker closest to the Indian mound was erected by one of Philippe's descendants, also his biographer, in an effort to correct what he calls the "historical inaccuracies" of the Philippe Park marker, erected in 1948. Although the Odet Philippe historical marker appears to mark his grave, his precise burial place is unknown (though somewhere on the former St. Helena's citrus plantation).

The controversy still brews, and whatever its outcome, Odet Philippe belies perceptions of Florida's early homesteaders being white farmers of limited means and education, eking out a living from the center of the state. One account describes Philippe as "dark as Alabama," Alabama being a household slave mentioned elsewhere in the account. Together with the now widely accepted theory of his Haitian heritage on his mother's side, bolstered by several well-documented portraits portraying Philippe as biracial, or of African descent, such early accounts demonstrate that this perception isn't always true.

BAHIA ESPIRITU SANTO MISSION

When Hernando De Soto discovered Tampa Bay just south of here on Pentecost Sunday in 1539, he named it Bahia Espiritu Sancto (Holy Spirit Bay). In 1567, a Spanish governor, Menéndez de Avilés, established a garrison of thirty soldiers here and empowered a Jesuit priest, Father Juan Rogel, to found a blockhouse mission that would be known as the Bahia Espiritu Santo Mission.

The priest peacefully evangelized 1,500 Tocobaga men over the course of several months. They seemed to accept Christianity and began to live peacefully with the Europeans. But when Father Rogel was called away from the mission for a brief time, he returned to find twenty-seven soldiers slain; the remaining three were slain when the Tocobagans saw Father

Rogel's ship returning. The mission was abandoned in 1568, and the Jesuits exited Florida for good in 1572. The Bahia Espiritu Santo Mission historical marker is located between the Philippe Park parking area and the harbor, at coordinates 28°0.605 N, 82°40.788 W. Bahia Espiritu Santo Mission Catholic Church, established in 1964, sits near the park entrance off Philippe Parkway.

12

JOHN'S PASS

A (STILL) UNSOLVED MYSTERY OF LOST GOLD

Caladesi Island and Clearwater Beach form the northern end of a stretch of tiny barrier islands off the coast of Pinellas County and boast some of the most beautiful beaches in Florida, with powdery white sand, brilliant sunsets, and crashing emerald waves. Pier 60 is the hub of Clearwater Beach, today densely populated, full of hotels, condominiums, and expensive parking meters. Intoxicated beach patrons partying too hard before the sun goes down can be a nuisance, and gang violence occasionally erupts, especially during Spring Break and Memorial Day weekends. Some postcard-worthy scenes are found here, but most head farther south past the pier for more mellow coastal landscapes.

Gulfview Boulevard leaves Clearwater Beach behind as it crosses the Sand Key Bridge to Sand Key, which is five miles in length and includes Belleair Beach and Indian Rocks Beach. Sand Key also houses the small municipalities of Redington Beach and Madeira Beach, ending at John's Pass where a drawbridge brings motorists to Treasure Island.

Today, John's Pass is a pirate-themed boardwalk lined with shops, ice cream parlors, and souvenir shops that have grown up around the perfect pirate's treasure narrative, too regionally beloved to be questioned:

> *It was late summer of 1848, and an old pirate named John Levique was returning to a familiar key off of La Florida after a voyage up to New Orleans (by some accounts Key West) to peddle his smoked turtle and*

turtle shells. His gunslinging days long past, this sweet old seadog turned turtle fisherman had staked a modest claim somewhere southeast of the barrier key today known as Treasure Island, on Boca Ciega Bay.

As a French peasant boy he'd worked on a Spanish galleon, but when his master's ship was captured by pirates he joined their crew in exchange for his life. He never amassed fortune because he was too friendly to hold his victims for ransom, much less make them walk the plank. He did manage to acquire a small chest of gold by the late 1840s, which supplemented his income as a turtle fisherman.

He'd buried his treasure off a small key he frequented, just before casting off for New Orleans (no pirate worth his salt would travel the Lonely Leg of La Florida with any kind of loot on his vessel). Upon returning, he surmised a scallywag of a squall had swept through and carved out a new pass to Boca Ciega, smack-dab on the spot where poor old John Levique had buried his gold. That same September 1848 hurricane that had stranded Philippe's family on the Indian burial mound up in Safety Harbor had destroyed the narrow peninsula where

Named for the mythical John Levique, a down-on-his-luck pirate who misplaced his loot after the epic hurricane of 1848, John's Pass Boardwalk lies on one of several inlets off Treasure Island near St. Petersburg. The 1848 superstorm created inlets and destroyed islands, including the one containing Old John's buried treasure. *Author photo.*

> *the pirate hid his cache. It probably still lies at the bottom of the Gulf of Mexico, and despite constant efforts by treasure hunters, has never been found.*

In losing his riches, Levique gained lasting standing as a folk hero of sorts, as the inlet now bears his name (in spite of the fact that no one is exactly sure of his real surname—he could neither read nor write and used an X as his signature).

The destiny of the Tampa Bay Metropolitan Area is intertwined with pirate lore, and pirate culture drives much of its identity, from the annual Gasparilla Parade each January to the mascot of Tampa's professional football team, the Tampa Bay Buccaneers. Old John Levique and John's Pass make their own artful contribution to the area's popular imagination, and a history punctuated with pirate tales, shipwrecks and buried treasure.

13
JUNGLE PRADA'S ANCIENT BURIAL GROUNDS

Overlooking Boca Ciega Bay, across from John's Pass and Treasure Island, sits the community of Jungle Terrace, and Jungle Prada de Narvaez Park. The large mound just south of the parking area was the dwelling of an Indian chief and was likely used for ceremonial purposes. Archaeologists named the mound the Jungle Prada Site; it's a nine-hundred-foot midden, or burial mound, where hundreds of human skeletons have been unearthed over the years. Today Jungle Prada is a City of St. Petersburg park, and visitors may walk among the small network of trails mounting the prehistoric man-made hill. (Visitors, though, are asked not to bother the peacocks, which are feral in this area, with local town hall meetings and newspaper editorials frequently witnessing a passionate debate—*Peacock: Nostalgic or Nuisance?*)

In 1926, developers constructed the low, Spanish-style JP Tavern, a restaurant and nightclub adjacent to Jungle Prada de Narvaez Park. Its curious name derives from the Prado Promenade in Cuba,[19] combined with the dense tropical vegetation found in this stretch of the Gulf Coast. Its original purpose was a row of shopping and entertainment storefronts, catering to the wealthy patrons of the Jungle Country Club Hotel, a half mile south on Park Street, now Admiral Farragut Academy. The extant brick road connecting Admiral Farragut and JP Tavern marks the remnant of the brick thoroughfare by which wealthy country club guests in Model-Ts drove out for fine dining, shopping, and entertainment from the hotel. At that time, Northerners wintering in Florida customarily arrived

Havana's Prado Promenade inspired the Jungle Prado on what later became known as the Jungle Prada Archeological Site. The original Jungle Prado building ("Prado" morphed into "Prada" in later years) is now home to a restaurant and nightclub. *State Archives of Florida.*

shortly after January 1, returning home for Easter, so hotels offered only monthly, never nightly rates. A place to shop and dine away from their accommodations enhanced the prospect of spending an entire month or more in a Florida "jungle."

However, the development project came with its share of skeletons in the closet—literally. In a memoir about the ups and downs of his Florida business projects, the original developer later admitted that the workers daily unearthed human skeletons during the 1926 construction project; they were of course working in the midst of an Indian midden. The Florida land boom ended right as the last stone was laid, and the Great Depression set in shortly thereafter. The luxury hotel became a boarding school, and the shopping and dining area closed for lack of business, changing hands a few times over the next several decades, no one owner ever sticking with the location for long.

Today, the century old three-hundred-foot building still sits atop hundreds of human skeletons, and historic preservation laws prevent the current owner from moving or updating the building, as this would further disturb the human remains. The result is a crumbling, dated building invoking the tacky opulence of a 1920s-era flappers and cigar social scene,

Jungle Prado developer unearthed a problem when he commenced construction of the Roaring Twenties entertainment district. Hundreds of human skeletons lay beneath the convenient "high place" on the coast of Boca Ciega Bay, which turned out to be an ancient burial mound of the Native Tocobaga tribe. *Author photo.*

with no updates or restoration in sight. It would seem that otherwise laudable historic preservation efforts seeking to protect culturally significant properties may have reached a point of diminishing returns on this particular site.

After exploring the Indigenous site and keeping a cordial distance from the peafowl, visitors may venture out onto the small boardwalk trail leading to the bay. Here in 1528 landed a lesser-known conquistador, Pánfilo de Narváez. With reddish blond hair, a huge frame, and a deep, resounding voice, he was apparently missing one eye, lost in a skirmish a few years prior to landing here. With him were four hundred men and forty horses, as well as six Franciscan friars and several Catholic priests. In five other ships, the wives of some of his men, along with more horses and supplies, were headed up the Gulf Coast hoping to meet the land party at a poorly defined harbor; this meeting never occurred.

Indeed, Narváez isn't as well known as Ponce de Leon and Hernando de Soto because of the abject failure of his conquest. The Tocobago Indians native to Pinellas County assured Narváez and his party that gold was to be found near modern-day Tallahassee. His party of four hundred got lost repeatedly as they sought to mine a precious metal on a peninsula composed entirely of sand and limestone. (The Tocobago chief who gave him directions to the gold mine near Tallahassee must have had a good laugh as he watched the caravan disappear into the swamp!)

After losing most of their men to disease, starvation, Indigenous aggression, and exhaustion and killing their own horses for food, Narváez was separated from the main party in a shipwreck. He was never heard from again. The survivors somehow eked out a livelihood as slaves, healers, and traders with Indigenous tribes in Texas, then eventually walked to the Pacific Ocean, becoming the first white men to cross the continent of North America. Just four men, including Álvar Núñez Cabeza de Vaca, finally reported their incredible story to the Spanish viceroy in Mexico, nearly a decade after embarking. De Vaca had kept diaries of the group's mishaps and struggles, which is how historians today know the tragic story of Narváez's failed conquest.

On this spot is the historical marker for the first Catholic Mass offered in Florida, a few feet north of the small marina. (Note: St. Augustine claims the distinction of site of the first Mass offered in Florida, and it is unclear which site merits the honor.) Narváez's entourage included several clergy, and the entire party paused on disembarking to offer thanksgiving prayers for the safe landing.

14
THE DON CESAR

A flipped coin—or else a short straw—named the city of St. Petersburg and, by extension, St. Pete Beach, the home of the "Pink Castle," The Don CeSar. One Peter Demens, a distant relative of Leo Tolstoy, won the lot against his cofounder in naming the southern terminus for the Orange Belt Railway, completed in 1888. Born to Russian nobility, Demens had come to America in 1881, arriving in New York City, and took the first train for his cousin's orange plantation in Jacksonville. Unable to afford Jacksonville land prices at the time, he boarded a steamboat headed for the backcountry, which brought him to Longwood, north of Orlando. He soon owned the mill that supplied the Orange Belt Railway with railway ties, which introduced him to the world of railroads. When the Orange Belt Railway was threatened to go under for lack of capital, Demens jumped at the opportunity and bought the company. (Henry B. Plant would later take the railroad off Demens's hands, making it a part of the Plant Railway.) The first train roared into its last depot, a remote barrier island with no sidewalks or roads and unnamed on any map. Demens and his partner cast lots for who would name this final whistlestop, and being a native of St. Petersburg, Russia, Demens picked "St. Petersburg."

It was the mid-1920s. Nearby on Boca Ciega, Fuller was enlarging his Jungle empire (only to discover he was building it on the remains of thousands of human skeletons at what is now known as the Jungle Prada archaeological site). The landscape's natural beauty was now accessible to Northern visitors arriving by way of train, yet the virginal beaches and tranquil gulf shoreline remained undeveloped. One of Fuller's visiting business associates remarked on the unique opportunity St. Petersburg offered to Northern developers. That was Thomas Rowe, who began scanning the sugary shoreline for the perfect location to begin construction on an idea of his own.

Starting with Jungle Prado as inspiration, Rowe decided to go bigger—and pinker—with a three-hundred-room hotel that could be seen from miles off the coast in the Gulf of Mexico. Architect Henry Dupont used a floating concrete pad and pyramid pilings for stability; even a century later, the structure has yet to shift in the notoriously soft and unreliable sands of the barrier key. Its architectural style borrows from Mediterranean and Moorish elements, blending the red tile roof, stucco walls, and tiled courtyards of the Spanish villa with the horseshoe arches, minarets, and complex stucco work of the mosque. Visits to boom-era Miami, Boca Raton, and St. Augustine—also blossoming playgrounds of the rich and famous in the early twentieth century—contributed to Rowe's vision. Rowe intended the splendid, lavish structure to be the crown jewel of a sprawling Mediterranean-style subdivision catering—like Jungle Prado—to the wealthiest snowbirds and their friends. January 1928 saw the grand opening of the hotel, attended by A-list guests like F. Scott Fitzgerald, Al Capone, Franklin Delano Roosevelt, and Lou Gehrig.

The story behind the hotel's name, Don CeSar, has intrigued guests and locals for the nearly a century.[20] Even skeptics agree that Rowe named his project after *Don César de Bazan*, a British opera playing on both sides of the Atlantic at the turn of the twentieth century. It is likely that Rowe witnessed the opera as a young student in Britain, and there is no doubt that it made a lasting impression.[21]

Controversy begins over the nature of this impression: local legend has it that Rowe fell in love with one Lucinda de Guzman, the star soprano playing the role of Maritana, the woman caught between two lovers in the opera. The young Thomas Rowe wanted to elope with Lucinda, the daughter of Spanish nobility, against her parents' wishes. On the night the young couple were to leave for America, Lucinda's parents intervened and brought her back to Spain, away from the longing heart of her American beau. Shortly thereafter, Lucinda died, writing Thomas a final note, bidding him farewell and imploring him to think of their love when he stood by the fountain. Apparently, a courtyard fountain was the rendezvous location for the beleaguered young couple, much in the style of *Romeo and Juliet.* Though Thomas married later, he never forgot his first love, and by the time he stood

The Don CeSar Hotel, St. Petersburg's "Pink Palace," was constructed in the Moorish tradition, an architectural trend in Roaring Twenties hotels. (Henry B. Plant's Tampa Bay Hotel and St. Augustine's Castle Warden are two others.) *"Don Cesar Hotel, St. Pete Beach" by porkfok6 CC 2.0.*

on the shores of St. Petersburg contemplating his hotel project, he had been estranged from his legal wife for many years.

Skeptics hold that Rowe indeed loved *Don César de Bazan* but question the piece about Lucinda and the lovers' tryst by the fountain. Fanning the flames of the intrigue were the circumstances of Lowe's untimely death: He suffered a fatal heart attack in the lobby of the Don CeSar, standing next to the hotel fountain. The circumstances of his death coupled with the account of Lucinda's final love letter to Thomas decades prior gave rise to reports of the couple meeting by the hotel lobby's fountain, finally fulfilling their love's desire, albeit from beyond the grave.

Evidence lends some truth to the tale, though I cannot speak to the authenticity of the ghostly appearances at the hotel fountain. An opera, even one's favorite opera, seems an odd choice for a hotel name, especially thirty years after the last curtain call. Something more than fondness for the stage appears to lurk beneath the surface of the name. Moreover, evidence suggests that Rowe's marriage to his legal wife, Mary Lucille, was an unhappy one: He left her nothing in his will, the couple had no children, and they had not spoken for years prior to his untimely death. This doesn't prove that Rowe's hotel was a tribute to his beloved Maritana, but the conclusion does seem to fit the known evidence.

Unfortunately, like Fuller's Jungle project, Rowe's Spanish-themed development arrived on the scene just in time to miss the boom. Florida sank into the Depression along with the rest of the nation by the close of the 1920s, and only the Don CeSar Hotel survived. When Rowe's life ended suddenly in 1940, his estranged wife took title to the Don CeSar, initiating a stage of neglect for the Pink Palace. The U.S. government purchased the hotel for a military hospital during World War II, but it faced demolition by the end of the 1960s.

In 1971, a group of locals united to "Save the Don,"[22] and the property revived due to a major restoration project under new ownership. By the 1980s, the Pink Palace had regained its former glory and was admitted to the National Register of Historic Places.

In 2015, Historic Hotels of America named the Don Cesar the "Best Historic Hotel in America."

15

EGMONT KEY LIGHTHOUSE

Between Anna Maria Island and Cabbage Key, home of DeSoto National Monument, lies a remote island, running north–south, measuring about two and a half miles long. It was first noticed by a British surveyor in 1765 and named in honor of John Perceval, the second Earl of Egmont.[23] The British held La Florida at this time due to the Treaty of Paris, in which Spain surrendered La Florida in exchange for Cuba and the Philippines, which the British had captured in the Seven Years' War. (Spain took Florida back in 1783 after just two decades of British possession.)

The lighthouse was constructed in 1848 as a much-needed navigational beacon, the only lighthouse between Key West and St. Mark's in the Panhandle. Prior to this time, West Florida was the site of numerous, often fatal shipwrecks.

Unfortunately, 1848 was the same year as the fateful hurricane that caused Odet Philippe to take refuge on the Indian burial mound in Safety Harbor and buried John Leverique's chest of gold at the bottom of the Gulf of Mexico, carving out John's Pass. Only months after the lighthouse's official certification in April 1848, the hurricane flooded Egmont Key, driving the lighthouse keeper and his family from the island. He resigned his post after only five months.

Tampa Bay is the lightning capital of the world, and constant strikes, plus a brief winter freeze or two in the 1850s, caused cracks in the tower that destabilized the lighthouse.

The keeper's log for that period describes the unseasonable cold that set in February 1852:

> *We have had ice here three-eighths of an inch thick, and the fish have been so chilled as to be unable to navigate. Numbers of them have been washed up on the beach—among which I saw several small shovel-nosed sharks. Our potatoes, watermelons, peppers, and most other vegetables are all killed. Amazing weather for this latitude.*[24]

A stronger, better replacement was erected in 1857, twice the height of the original. Recall that the original was constructed to assist mariners traversing the route from Key West to St. Mark's in the Panhandle. During the Civil War, the Egmont Key light was caught in the middle—literally—of the conflict between the North and the South. The lighthouse on Key West, also home to a U.S. Army and U.S. Navy stronghold, remained loyal to the Union, whereas the St. Mark's Lighthouse in the Panhandle sided with the Confederacy, along with the rest of the state. Both the Union and the Confederacy engaged in varying levels of sabotage of lighthouses along Florida's coastline during the Civil War, with lighthouse keepers often stuck, as it were, between a rock and, well, a lighthouse! In 1861, Keeper Rickard pretended loyalty to the Union when the Union blockade officers were passing through but quickly packed up the Fresnel (pronounced fre-NEL) lens and escaped to Tampa as soon as the Unionists disappeared around Cabbage Key.

Strategically darkening the lamps of key lighthouse stations along Florida's often treacherous coastline made navigation next to impossible, and lighthouse keepers—usually Southern sympathizers—worked closely with blockade runners to extinguish the lamps at just the right time, only to reignite the flames when the blockade runners approached the harbor. The Florida coastline occupies a mighty chunk of General Winfield Scott's so-called Anaconda, the plan by which he blockaded Confederate ports, squeezing and starving the South into submission. A few darkened beacons along the coast when the blockade vessel approached meant disaster for the Union mariners attempting to navigate unfamiliar waters in total darkness.

The second Egmont Key Lighthouse (1857) still stands today. In more recent years, its upkeep has been the special project of the Tampa Bay Rough Riders, a service organization founded in honor of President Teddy Roosevelt's volunteer cavalry regiment with roots in Tampa. Local volunteers

For many years, Egmont Key—named for the second Earl of Egmont—was home to the sole navigational beacon between Key West and St. Marks in the Panhandle. Prior to the light's construction in 1857, constant shipwrecks plagued Florida's treacherous west coast. *State Archives of Florida.*

decorate the lighthouse with Christmas lights, and the historic lighthouse has many friends and admirers from the mainland.

The lighthouse can be seen from the end of the Fishing Pier at Fort De Soto Park on Tierra Verde. The pier is crowded with fishermen at any hour of the day, and it would be unusual *not* to see a dolphin from this pier. From the end of the pier, Egmont Key is the strip of green land viewed across the bay in a west–southwesterly direction. Today all that remains on the two-and-a-half-mile island is a crumbling fort and the lighthouse (and the park ranger's residence).

FORT DE SOTO RUINS

Fort De Soto was constructed in 1898 at the entrance of Tampa Bay to protect Tampa's residents from Spanish aggression during the Spanish-American War. Today, Fort De Soto is known best for its in-demand campground and its beautiful beaches. A well-appointed Quartermaster Storehouse Museum, housed in a careful reconstruction of the original building, documents the short settlement that grew up here around Fort De Soto, including lively biographies of the officers' wives and how they dealt with the heat, the mosquitoes, and the rain.

Heading toward the historic fort ruins, a ramp ascends the mound on its western side and then descends on the other side. Here a path circles back east to the inner parade gallery, where visitors can access the cool inner chambers of the fortress—and find themselves in total darkness if the corridors are followed deeply enough.

16

PASS-A-GRILLE

A STUDY IN PASTELS

After passing the Don CeSar, visitors arrive at the bubblegum-pink beach town of Pass-a-Grille on the southern tip of St. Pete Beach, formerly known as Long Island. Its unusual name is part of the charm of this whimsical coastal village with a Bohemian meets Cape Cod culture. It likely derives from a French expression, *passe aux grilleurs*, meaning, "grillers' pass." This narrow strip of sand may have been where the Conchs of Key West and other fishermen rested for the night en route to Anclote Key or New Orleans, to grill the catch of the day. It also could have been where John Devique instructed turtlers to enter the bay to reach his fish smoking camp, somewhere on Boca Ciega Bay. He may have named the channel Grillers' Pass because he used an iron grate, or grille, over an open fire, to smoke his customers' dinner. Soon the self-styled "last of the pirates" John Gomez (the same bilge rat who spared the life of Odet Philippe in exchange for his medical knowledge) began ferrying tourists from Tampa, making Pass-a-Grille one of Florida's first resort towns.

At the corner of Pass-a-Grille Way and Eighth Avenue is the Seahorse Restaurant (1938). A meal at the Seahorse is a miniature course in local history: The tabletops are covered in newspaper clippings and postcards from Pass-a-Grille's lighthearted past. The Seahorse's décor also pays tribute to Mrs. Beasely, the town dog, who was affectionately fed and occasionally housed by residents in the 1990s and lives on as a kind of informal town mascot. That's the kind of town Pass-a-Grille is: even a stray dog becomes a charming part of local lore. Nearby is Pass-a-Grille's "downtown," which is basically Eighth Avenue, experienced best on foot. Ripley of *Ripley's Believe It or Not* fame once called Pass-a-Grille's Eighth Avenue "America's shortest and most beautiful main street."[25]

One lot west of the Seahorse is the historical marker for Zephaniah Phillips, Pass-a-Grille's first homesteader. Captain Z. Phillips arrived in Illinois from Toronto when he was less than two years old. He was a Civil War veteran, and his discharge form dated 1851 describes him as "6' in height, dark complexion, grey eyes, black hair and by profession when enrolled, a carriage-maker."[26] His obituary notes that he brought his family to the Pinellas Peninsula in 1885 after settling briefly in North Florida. Zephaniah and his two sons, Zephaniah Jr. and Clarence, built a boat, called *Silver Moon*, with which they hauled lumber for the construction of their home. Captain Phillips and his wife, Mary, are buried in Greenwood Cemetery near downtown St. Petersburg. In 2013, Zephaniah's wood-frame cottage was moved here from its original location just a block south, at the intersection of Pass-a-Grille Way and Seventh Avenue. Today, its original location is occupied by a block of colorful three-story condominiums.

Historic bungalows and coastal cottages line tiny Pass-a-Grille's main street, including Pass-a-Grille General Store, located in a 1908 wood-frame bungalow formerly known as the Judge Schwerdtfeber house. *Author photo.*

A block north sits the eclectic Pass-a-Grille General Store at 808 Pass-a-Grille Way. Housed in a well-appointed 1908 wood-frame bungalow formerly known as the Judge Schwerdtfeber House, the general store is more of a boutique offering trendy coastal décor, bath products, and apparel in addition to old-fashioned sweets and some dry goods.

A block west of Pass-a-Grille Way is the Gulf Beaches Historical Museum, located in a former church built in 1917. Its purpose is to "collect, preserve and exhibit the history of the barrier islands," and the museum is staffed entirely by volunteers. Keystone Motel, located back on Eighth where it ends at Gulf Way, is a proven, affordable, family-owned beach motel in business since 1945. Castle Hotel, founded in 1906, is located at the corner of Fourth Avenue and Gulf Way; the lobby and a few of the guest rooms are original. At least twenty other historical cottages and bungalows are preserved on Pass-a-Grille. (My personal favorite is 105 Fourth Street, formerly a one-room schoolhouse.) FloridaTraveler.org offers an excellent free online guide to these historic residences.[27]

17

A CIGAR MAKER'S STORY

YBOR CITY

Vicente Martinez-Ybor[28] was born in Valencia, Spain, in 1818 and moved to the Spanish colony of Cuba at the age of fourteen. Prior to leaving his native land, Vicente learned the art of cigar-rolling from an elderly man, a fellow worker at the grocery store at which Vicente was employed.

Once in the Spanish colony of Cuba, Vicente opened a cigar factory, producing at one point over twenty thousand cigars a day. At this time in Cuba, the movement for independence from Spain strengthened, and Vicente was an ardent supporter of the cause. Because of his allegiance to the cause for independence, Vicente came under persecution and moved his operation to Key West, already a well-known producer of Cuban cigars. Eventually, even Key West became politically unwelcoming to the likes of Vicente, and he began to cast about for a new location for his ever-popular hand-rolled product.

At about this time, another Spanish entrepreneur was casting about, but his object was guava. Though a civil engineer by trade, Gavino Gutierrez was employed by a fruit-packing company in New York, which had tasked him with selecting a crop for a new product line. In his wanderings, Gutierrez traveled through Florida, a rough journey in the late 1880s when oxcarts bumped unsteadily over soft sand, mucky swamps, and malaria-infested bogs. When he finally arrived in Key West, he encountered Ybor, and the two businessmen hit it off. Gutierrez had come across the military outpost of Fort Brooke in his travels and had noted the semitropical climate and pleasant aspect of the tiny town where the Hillsborough River emptied into the protected Bahia Spiritu Sancto (today known as Tampa Bay) and then the Gulf of Mexico. The military presence coupled with Henry B. Plant's new railway system spurred a nascent economy that might make the perfect spot for Ybor's newest endeavor.

Gutierrez never found his guava plants, but his mind was on other things. He joined Ybor in the new venture, opening a cigar factory just outside of Tampa. The industry flourished here due to Ybor City's ideal location; its proximity to Cuba meant quick and easy imports of Cuban tobacco, its humid climate kept the tobacco leaves soft and pliant, and Plant's new railway afforded convenient transportation of the product to New York City and the rest of the world. By 1886, Gutierrez and Ybor were operating the largest cigar factory in the world, occupying one full city block. Today, the original Ybor Cigar Factory still stands on Thirteenth Street in Ybor City, at its intersection with Eighth and Ninth Avenues. Controversially, this, Ybor City's defining edifice, was purchased in 2010 by the Church of Scientology, whose headquarters are in nearby Clearwater in Pinellas County.

Other cigar factory owners from Key West in Cuba moved in shortly thereafter, and a thriving economy emerged based mainly on the everyday needs of workers. Until the late 1890s, most of Ybor's employees were seasonal; they considered Key West or Cuba their home and traveled back and forth to Ybor City to work a season in the factory. Yet Ybor realized a commuting population would never provide a reliable workforce, so he sought to build a company town much like the manufacturing and mining towns in the North. He built inexpensive housing for his employees, which he sold them at cost. These tiny wooden houses came to be known as shotgun houses due to their layout: a bullet shot from the front door could exit unscathed through an open back door due to a hallway stretching the length of the structure. Off this main hallway were usually a small living room, a bedroom, and finally a kitchen. The back door exit from the kitchen rear wall of the hallway led to the outhouse in the backyard.

Simultaneous to Ybor's decision to erect a company town of shotgun houses, known as *casitas* to the cigar makers, Key West, already overcrowded, experienced the devastating fire of 1896. The flames destroyed most structures in Key West, driving thousands of working-class Cuban émigrés from their homes and jobs. As a result, Ybor City was flooded with homeless but willing workers from Key West, with knowledge of cigar rolling and in desperate need of gainful employment. The result was a perfect storm for Ybor's new town: Ybor City exploded with growth at the turn of the twentieth century.

The highly skilled cigar makers, known as *tabaqueros*, were apprenticed with more experienced cigar rollers before attaining permanent positions in the best factories. Their roles were shaped more like Old World cottage industries and small village artisans than by conventional Industrial Age factory norms. Moreover, the cigar rollers in factories like Ybor's were relatively well educated for their time: Regular readers, or *lectores*, were employed by the factory owners to read aloud while others rolled cigars. Newspapers, magazines, literary journals, advertisements, and fiction and nonfiction texts were broadcast to the cigar workers as they went about their craft.

At five o'clock in the afternoon, the tabaquero would leave the factory and head back to his casita or the boardinghouse where he stayed. On the way, he might stop by a saloon for a quick shot of booze before arriving at his room. Every cigar worker, man or woman, bathed immediately after work. The smell of tobacco was potent, and hands and fingers, nail beds, and even clothes and hair were permeated with the strong odor of tobacco leaves. A long bath, likely in a washtub, removed the odors from skin and hair. A fresh set of clothes was donned, and the young cigar man was ready for an evening of drinking, playing cards, dancing, or socializing with his fellow workers.[29] Cafés, meetinghouses, social clubs, saloons, drugstores, and gaming houses sprouted up like weeds amid the more than three hundred factories in Ybor City and West Tampa in the cigar-making heyday of the 1920s.

In the same vein, a cottage industry of cigar boxes evolved, as the coveted hand-rolled product required sound housing for its journey to the ultimate consumer in Chicago, New York City, and beyond. The evolution of the cigar box—and vibrant cigar label—became as boutique and highly specialized as that of a good Cuban cigar. The primary producer of the collectible cedar boxes with their red, green, and yellow hues, often framed by verdant palms and featuring smiling Spanish ladies, was the Tampa Box Company. Cigar box historians report that to this day, an old-timer in Shanghai, Moscow, or Munich might use a Tampa Box Company cigar box to hold his petty cash behind the counter.

So many cigars were exported from Florida in the first half of the twentieth century: the whole world knew the best tobacco leaves came from Cuba and were almost always rolled in Tampa, Florida cigar shops.

At its height in 1919, Ybor City rolled around four and a half million cigars annually.

The cottage industry dwindled in the 1930s with the invention of cigar-rolling machines, though the authentic, hand-rolled product was still a popular choice. But in the 1950s and 1960s, the federal government initiated a program of urban renewal in Tampa's historic Latin Quarter, which most locals agree was an abject failure. The vibrant multicultural spirit of Vicente Ybor's town was smothered by government housing and, the nail in the coffin, the construction of the behemoth eight-laned Interstate 4 (completed in 1964). The federal government's activities coincided with Fidel Castro's Communist regime in Cuba, and the embargo on imports of tobacco disrupted the production of Ybor City's defining cottage industry. Cigar manufacturers scrambled to import tobacco leaves from the Dominican Republic, Puerto Rico, and elsewhere, but the hand-rolled Cuban cigar magic was gone forever.

By the 1980s and 1990s, most factories had closed, and accessory industries supporting the cigar culture, like cafés, bars, and culture clubs, also faced closures. Street crime rose precipitously as gangs moved in, and family-run business and homes exited.

The twenty-first century ushered in a period of gentrification though, which Ybor City observers and Latin Quarter historic preservationists generally consider a good thing. Cigar factories in the historic district that survived the urban renewal of the 1960s are now tenanted by tech start-ups, art galleries, internet cafés, and professional offices. Most of the structures are protected by historic preservation laws, and the city is finding itself on the up-and-up after four decades of steady decline.

The Columbia

Several landmark businesses and establishments survived the decline in the 1950s and 1960s and continue to serve Ybor City to the present day. The Columbia has been in continuous operation since Spaniard Casimiro Hernandez opened it as a humble saloon in 1905 at the corner of Twenty-Second and Ybor City's main street, Seventh Avenue.[30] At first, the Columbia was a corner bar serving drinks to cigar workers after work or a café con leche and Cuban toast for a midday repast. Even when Florida's Prohibition laws banned the sale of alcohol in 1918, followed by the Great

Depression in the 1930s, the Columbia managed to hold on through the tough times where other businesses failed. Ybor City's proximity to the Port of Tampa meant ready access to bootlegged alcohol smuggled in from the Caribbean, and Hernadez's great-great-grandchildren, who still own and operate the restaurant today, freely admit their family patriarch furnished libations to the working-class immigrant community continuously during Prohibition.[31]

With the repeal of Prohibition laws in 1933, the Columbia took on new life and new ownership in the person of Hernadez's son Casimiro Jr. Casimiro Jr. envisioned a more glamorous experience than a corner café and bar, with flamenco dancers, live bands, and champagne—or at least sangria. During this time of renewal, the Hernandez family installed the still impressive Don Quixote room, a lavish themed dining area surrounded by hand-painted tilework featuring scenes and features from Cervantes' 1605 Spanish novel. The Columbia continued to expand while remaining in the hands of the original Casimiro Hernadez family, with five immensely popular and beloved Florida locations from St. Augustine to Clearwater. Today, the 1905 salad prepared tableside blends chopped iceberg, anchovy, lemon, garlic, olive oil,

The Ferlita family arrived in Ybor City even before its namesake and opened Ferlita Bakery in 1833. The original building burned in 1925, but this new one was constructed in 1926. Today it is home to the Ybor City Museum. *"Ybor City Museum State Park" by Peter K. Burian CC BY-SA 4.0.*

tomato, Spanish ham, and swiss cheese, named for the year of its opening. A generous hunk of Cuban bread wrapped in white paper and a café con leche make this Columbia's most popular dish. Another favorite is the black bean cakes with guacamole, besides, of course, the *arroz con pollo*.

LA JOVEN FRANCESCA BAKERY (*The Young French Woman* Bakery) is the oldest business in Ybor City, predating even the advent of Vicente Ybor and Gavino Gutierrez in the 1890s. Prior to the transformation into the Cigar City, Sicilians arrived in the area east of the tiny fishing village and military outpost of *Tampa* and erected a few small homes and businesses here near the bayshore. One such Italian early arrival was Francesco Ferlita,[32] who opened this tiny bakery in 1833. Adapting to the changing customer base, the Ferlita family learned to speak Spanish and bake Cuban bread, as the unknown fishing hamlet became the bustling Cuban Cigar City. The original building was burnt in 1925 but was rebuilt, and today the 1926 bakery, known as the Ferlita Bakery, is home to the Ybor City Museum. An authentic *casita* sits adjacent to Ferlita's on Ninth Avenue in the heart of the Latin Quarter.

Churches and synagogues are noticeably absent from the Ybor City Historic District, and local code does not permit places of worship within Ybor City's historic district.[33] This marks a departure from other ethnic communities in older, established American cities, which usually pride themselves on their religious heritage. An anticlerical sentiment related to the Cuban liberation movement explains this absence, as well as the dominance of cultural clubs and mutual-aid societies, which took the place of Sunday morning worship for Ybor's first residents.[34] Even to this day, cultural clubs and mutual-aid societies represent the multinational cast of characters that founded and built Ybor City, most founded near the turn of the last century. L'Unione Italiana (Italian), Union Marti-Maceo (Afro-Cuban), Centro Espanol (Spanish), and the German-American Club (German) have all withstood the changing times, though some are dedicated to non-club-related activities in the present day.[35] For example, Centro Espanol became Centro Ybor, housing a brewery, bars, restaurants, and a gaming arcade; the German-American Club is now a county health center. Originally begun in the early 1900s, many of these groups held their principal meetings on Sunday mornings, a time traditionally reserved for family attendance at a worship service. This undercurrent of social unity and national ties superseding religious ties continues to define Ybor City and, to a lesser extent, the broader West Tampa culture.

18

BUNGALOW TERRACE OF OLD HYDE PARK

Nineteen colorful historic bungalows overlook a shady pedestrian byway in Hyde Park, one of Tampa's oldest neighborhoods.[36] At the time of the plat's recording, a bougainvillea-laden pergola shaded the sidewalk, imbuing the stone walkway with a charming ambience. Indeed, the 1906 plat includes the word *pergola* as part of the tiny subdivision's original plan. The pergola succumbed to the elements after the 1950s, but twin pylons at both the north and south entrances of the terrace are intact.

High-density residential South Tampa belies its agrarian roots circa 1900. Back in 1886, O.H. Platt purchased twenty acres from original Tampa settler Robert Jackson's homestead, when the total population of Tampa was only seven hundred. Platt named his acquisition Hyde Park, after the one on the southside of Chicago, by the shores of Lake Michigan. The west bank of the Hillsborough River was quite rural, with just a few orange groves and accompanying estates. The east bank of the Hillsborough River was the site of Fort Brooke, not extant. Then in 1888, Henry B. Plant constructed his Moorish Tampa Bay Hotel, today the University of Tampa, on the western bank of the Hillsborough River. The Kennedy Street Bridge, constructed the same year, opened access to the remote far edge of the Hillsborough River; prior to this time, a single ferry was the only means of accessing what is today known as Hyde Park and West Tampa. In 1893, the *Tampa Morning Tribune* called Hyde Park Tampa's "most aristocratic area."

Colonel Alfred Swann, a wealthy Tennessean and war hero, arrived on the scene in 1910 and purchased sixty acres from another early Tampa settler, William A. Morrison. Morrison's original home, an 1879 Italianate mansion, still stands on New Port Avenue in present-day Hyde Park. When developer Colonel Swann set his sights on this area, Morrison's place was still entirely surrounded by groves. Platt, Morrison, and Swann are all commemorated in the names of major avenues cutting through the heart of Tampa's oldest and most coveted residential neighborhoods: Hyde Park, Palma Ceia, Bayshore Boulevard, and Swann Estates.

Subdividing the citrus plantation into homesites, Colonel Swann called his development Suburb Beautiful. He and his partner, Eugene Holtsinger, began filling the mudflats along Hillsborough Bay and constructed a seawall along the bayshore. Today, Bayshore Boulevard is an iconic row of historic mansions and boasts the second-longest sidewalk in the continental United States, measuring four and a half miles in length.

Bungalow Terrace in Hyde Park appears much the same as it did at Tampa's inception in the early 1900s, when a developer successfully brought a Pasadena trend out of India—the bungalow—to Central Florida. The bungalow has one story, a wide porch, and exposed rafters and may have a "camel back," a small upper level that is always noticeably smaller than its lower level. *State Archives of Florida/Shriver.*

Tampa Land Company platted Bungalow Terrace in 1916 as four rows of one- or two-story homes on nineteen of the original thirty-one lots overlooking the still extant pedestrian terrace. The bungalow as an architectural style is defined by a gently pitched roof, large veranda, and natural material like wood shingles and brick or stone columns; exposed rafters complete the look. The bungalow's second story is dubbed a "camelback" due to the relatively small square footage of the upper level, evoking the hump of a camel. *Bungalow* originated in India and means simply a low residential structure with an oversized porch. The California firm Green and Green introduced the American bungalow in Pasadena around the beginning of the twentieth century.

Thereafter, the bungalow was billed as an affordable, trendy alternative to more classic traditional architectural residences, like the stately Queen Anne or the somber white columns of the Neoclassical Revival. The Hyde Park bungalow rose steadily in popularity between 1916 and 1933, extending far beyond the formal boundaries of Bungalow Terrace or even Hyde Park. Until this time, the only residences available to buyers of more moderate income were shotgun houses, and those were usually reserved for the servants of the larger estates. (Most of the original historic shotgun houses in and around West Tampa today were first inhabited by servants of the owners of the historic mansions, most of which are also still extant.) Although new construction of bungalows declined in popularity in the 1930s, plenty remain in and among the residential neighborhoods of Hyde Park, Tampa Heights, and even Bayshore Boulevard.

Residential development of the western bank of the Hillsborough River may have begun in Old Hyde Park, but it soon expanded westward all the way to the far side of the peninsula, its western shore. Indeed, the wealthiest, most exclusive residences in the City of Tampa cluster between these twin bookends of Westshore and Bayshore Boulevards. Hyde Park's shady streets, generous lawns, historic homes, and original brick roads define many West Tampa neighborhoods, platted around the turn of the last century, their original architecture and unmistakable character still palpable in the second quarter of the twenty-first century.

19

SPANISHTOWN CREEK

WHERE TAMPA BEGAN

Hernando de Escalante Fontaneda was a boy of thirteen when the Calusa tribe of southwestern Florida took him captive after his older brother's vessel ran ashore on the rocky shoals somewhere in the Florida Keys. Every other man on the ship was sacrificed, but young Hernando managed to make himself useful to the *cacique*, the Spanish word for the Native American chief, whom Hernando later called "King Carlos."

For the next seventeen years, Hernando wandered the peninsula of La Florida, and his 1575 memoir is the first known mention of the Calusa name Tanpa.

> *I will name over the villages and towns of the deceased cacique Carlos, who was put to death by sentence of the Captain Reynoso. First, a place called Tanpa, a large town, and another town, which is called Tomo.... Besides these there are others inland on the Lake of Mayaimi.*[37]

Later, a 1695 Spanish map shows *B. Tampa* where Tampa Bay presently lies; *B. Carlos* labels present-day Charlotte Harbor, the modern name thus deriving from young Hernando's word for the Calusa tribal chief. Historians maintain that the large town of Tanpa mentioned in the above account was actually Punta Gorda and the earliest Spanish maps confused Charlotte Harbor and Tampa Bay due to geographic similarities. Both Tampa and Charlotte Bay are deep-water harbors at the mouths of prominent southwestern-flowing rivers, partially enclosed by a peninsula and barrier keys.

Between the early 1780s and 1821, Cuban fishermen of Spanish descent, called *ranchos*, began arriving at Tampa Bay and Charlotte Harbor, making their homes along the creeks and tributaries feeding into the Hillsborough and Peace Rivers. The fishing was excellent along these shores, and the ranchos often brought their families and settled here permanently. They caught ample mullet, pompano, redfin, and trout to feed their households; excess was salted, dried, and sent back to Cuba for profit.

A cluster of six or seven families comprised the first non-Native settlement in Tampa, which came to be called Spanishtown Creek. Old plat maps of early subdivisions in Hyde Park show a creek originating near where the Selmon Expressway today crosses West Horatio Street. The creek winds its way southeast, crossing Magnolia Avenue, West Bay Street, and Bayshore Boulevard before emptying into Hillsborough Bay. In 1910, the City of Tampa began filling and building over Spanishtown Creek, eventually incorporating it into the municipal stormwater system. A fascinating study[38] conducted by an archaeologist for the Florida Public Archeology Network uses current Hyde Park maps overlaid with a former plat map, circa 1890, showing how Spanishtown Creek coincided with present-day stormwater drains. Spanishtown Creek, the genesis of the city of Tampa, the study concludes, still flows beneath Hyde Park as it did in the era of the Cuban ranchos.

In 1821, Florida became a U.S. territory, and the federal government interested itself in controlling and containing the presence of Florida's Native tribes, especially the Seminoles. By this time, disease had all but decimated Hernando de Escalante's Calusa tribe, which had populated the Gulf Coast for more than one thousand years. To accomplish this end, the United States built a fort at the mouth of the Hillsborough River on Tampa Bay. Fort Brooke would assist in enforcing the terms of a treaty recently signed with the Seminoles, in which they agreed to relocate to Central Florida, leaving coastal Florida free to development and settlement by Americans eager to trade with Caribbean nations. It was the English-speaking soldiers stationed at Fort Brooke who met and befriended the Spanish-speaking ranchos, dubbing the tiny village Spanishtown. Thatched palmetto huts sheltered the ranchos, who wove baskets of palm branches and fished the creek.

The Spanishtown Creek historical marker sits on the south side of West Bay Street, near its intersection with Bayshore Boulevard above the stormwater inlet draining into the bay.

20

SULPHUR SPRINGS WATER TOWER

The Sulphur Springs Water Tower (1921) is visible from downtown Tampa, Tampa Heights, Temple Terrace, Riverhills, Busch Gardens, Carrollwood, and the University of South Florida.[39] The Gothic Revival structure stands higher than any Florida lighthouse at 214 feet. Looming above the Hillsborough River snaking by at its base, the water tower has become an iconic part of the Tampa city skyline. Many stages of the story of Tampa coalesce here at the water tower, and a study of the springs and their tower is a study of the rhythm of the city and its residents.

The 59-mile Hillsborough River originates deep in the Green Swamp, near present-day Zephyrhills, and empties into Tampa Bay in Downtown Tampa. The name, Hillsborough, is for the Earl of Hillsborough, the British secretary of the Colony of West Florida. (Note: the Hillsborough River and Hillsborough County lie entirely within the historic British Colony of *East* Florida.) Interestingly, locals claim an actual lighthouse stood on this place in the Spanish era, to guide ranchos, pirates, and explorers along the dark channels of the unknown, uncharted Hillsborough River. Standing at 137 feet tall, the Hillsboro Inlet Lighthouse (1907), located in Pompano Beach in Brevard County and also named after the Earl of Hillsborough, presents an interesting contrast to the Sulphur Springs Water Tower, its "west coast" cousin.

The typical municipal water tower is a study in the bland, the utilitarian, and the drab. Its height pressurizes the stored water, ensuring a sufficient flow in times of limited or low water capacity to the citizens. A skeletal metal base supporting the tank acting as the reservoir and the pump assembly are common, the most interesting (if it can be called) aspect being lettering of the town name and maybe a local mascot or symbol.

Not so with developer Josiah Richardson's white stucco masterpiece, resembling a hybrid of a lighthouse and a medieval tower. Engineer Grover Poole included lancet windows, crenelated parapet walls, and scrolled footings. The tower's walls are eight-foot-thick poured concrete, and the tower sits atop a forty-five-foot foundation. At the base of the white tower is the natural spring that runs into the Hillsborough River.

Many other natural springs used to dot edges of the Hillsborough, most of which have been tapped to increase flow to other springs, thus strengthening the water pressure for residents of the area. Sulphur Spring withstood the infrastructure and population explosion of the 1900s, likely due to the presence of its iconic tower.

Located about five miles north of Downtown Tampa, Sulfur Spring appears in 1882 U.S. Land Office map, near another, smaller spring

Described as a cross between a lighthouse and a medieval tower, the Sulphur Springs Water Tower constructed by eccentric developer Josiah Richardson in 1927 flanks the Hillsborough River and the natural spring whose name it bears. *Courtesy of the River Tower Foundation.*

called John Swingley Spring. Today the John Swingley Spring is known as Purity Spring, and a small municipal park of the same name has grown up around it.

Sulphur Spring's first non-Native settler was a German pioneer and blacksmith named John Henry Krause, who lived and worked in Tampa but in 1882 purchased 170 acres of land north of Tampa for a second home. Later, Dr. John Mills arrived from the Netherlands, settling on what is now Lake Carroll, west of Sulphur Springs. In 1899, Mills purchased 90 acres from Krause, including the spring. Its rumored healing properties and the ongoing myth of the real fountain of youth popular at this time may have spurred the physician to purchase this particular tract. The *Tampa Tribune* reports on September 14, 1899, that "Dr. Mills says that in order to be perfectly safe from a dangerous fever, everybody should take a bath daily in Sulphur Springs." A restaurant, dancing pavilion, and numerous bathhouses had been added to the property by 1904.

Kentucky native Josiah Richardson borrowed $10,000 to purchase Dr. Mills's property when the latter and his wife moved into Tampa to operate a drugstore. At this time, visitors to Sulphur Springs from Tampa had to come by horse-drawn buggy, boat, or foot. Later, in 1907 a streetcar line connected downtown Tampa with Sulphur Springs. By 1910, Sulphur Springs was being billed as an "amusement park" with bowling, motion pictures, billiards, and a roller coaster, in addition to swimming and boating. In 1925, Richardson began construction of the Sulphur Springs Arcade, which Ripley's Believe It or Not! called an entire city under one roof; later it was dubbed America's first indoor shopping mall. The Sulphur Springs Hotel and Apartments opened in the 1930s, and Richardson's friends and enemies alike agreed the real estate man had struck gold. By this time, the spring had become so popular that a residential community began to sprout up north of Richardson's development, as North Tampa transformed from remote cow pasture to suburban neighborhood.

In 1927, Richardson mortgaged the entire Sulphur Springs property for $180,000 to finance the construction of his most dramatic development yet: the Sulphur Springs Water Tower. The arcade (what we'd today call an indoor mall) and other buildings at Sulphur Springs required more water than the spring itself could provide, necessitating additional reserves to keep business booming and customers happy.

Unfortunately, the gold mine didn't last forever. A September 1933 hurricane brought dramatic rainfall, bursting several dams and flooding

Richardson's Sulphur Springs compound. The arcade, the hotel and apartments, the amusement park and bathing houses, and the burgeoning residential area all sustained severe damage from the flooding, requiring total restoration to resume business. The onslaught of the Great Depression eroded business, and Richardson's huge mortgage, close to $3 million after inflation, became impossible for him to pay. He was forced to sell the entire Sulphur Springs estate to a tobacco farmer from South Carolina, J.F. Hendrick. Under Hendrick's management, Sulphur Springs roared back in the 1940s and 1950s, and Tampa's middle-class families continued to patronize the hotel and recreational amenities into the 1960s.

The 1970s were a period of true decline. The construction of Interstate 275 (1967), like Interstate 4 in Ybor City, permanently blighted the neighborhood. The City of Tampa forced the water tower out of operation in 1971 and neglected the tower and the springs for several decades thereafter. A drug culture still plaguing central Tampa set into Sulphur Springs in the 1970s and 1980s; the arcade was demolished in 1975 to make room for parking for dog tracks. In 1988, Sherwin Williams donated 150 gallons of "graffiti-proof" white paint to refresh the structure.

Today the former Sulphur Springs compound is home to a city park and a public pool built in 2003; the pool closed in 2023 for concerns about cracks in its foundation and public safety. The City of Tampa estimates repairs will cost around $10 million. No plan to commence repair work has been announced as of this writing.

SOUTHWEST CENTRAL

BRADENTON TO CHARLOTTE HARBOR

21

DE SOTO'S LANDFALL AND ANNA MARIA ISLAND

Hernando de Soto sailed past the seven-mile barrier island of Anna Maria in May 1539 to the mouth of the Manatee River, where he made landfall at approximately the site of DeSoto National Monument in Bradenton (formerly *Braiden-town*). He and an army of six hundred men set out to explore the interior of the southeastern United States.[40]

Although DeSoto's trail is still being precisely mapped, a 1988 study commissioned by the U.S. Parks Service concludes that he did not stay long. Finding the sandy terrain barren and inhospitable, he skirted the shore of Snead Island, unloading horses and men at approximately present-day Port Manatee to lighten his ships. He continued north to the mouth of the Little Manatee River, where he cautiously entered Cockroach Bay, mindful of his predecessors' deadly clashes with Native residents. De Soto set up camp at the mouth of the Manatee River on its north shore, in an Indian village he later identified as Ocita. Here he found Juan Ortiz, a kidnapped Spaniard who had lived with a local tribe for more than a decade. Ortiz acted as a valuable guide and translator for De Soto in his journey eastward, following present-day US-301 from around Wimauma north to Bushnell and then up US-41 to Tallahassee. The definitive study thus far on the 1539 route, commissioned by the National Park Service and completed in 1988, suggests that they crossed the Withlacoochee River in Bushnell, close to the Dade National Battlefield Historic Site. De Soto's party continued into Georgia and the southeastern United States, where he died of a fever just three years later at the age of forty-three. De Soto's precise location of death is not known, but the NPS study places it somewhere in Louisiana, on the banks of the Mississippi River, south of its confluence with the Arkansas River.

In 1757, when Don Francisco Maria Celi mapped the Bahia Spiritu Sancto, he used Egmont Key as a point of reference and called Anna Maria Island, *Punta Arboleda*, meaning "Grove Point."[41] Nearly a decade later, an 1862 Spanish map labels this barrier island *Cayo Ana Maria* after the Blessed Virgin Mary and her mother, St. Ann. Later Tampa Mayor Madison Post "named" the key after his wife, Maria, and his sister-in-law, Anna. However, the Spanish map appellation was likely already commonly known even to speakers of English. Post, a Confederate deputy marshal and a passionate defender of the institution of slavery, was also a well-known anti-Catholic; thus the naming of his new island after his wife and sister-in-law may have been more palatable to him than validating the Spanish-Catholic reference.

Anna Maria Island (note that old-timers emphasize its fourth syllable, elongating the vowel resulting in *A-nuh-mar-EYE-ah*) is home to three separate towns: from north to south, the city of Anna Maria (1922), the city of Holmes Beach (1950), and the city of Bradenton Beach (1953).

Mayor Post and his family didn't settle Anna Maria, but numerous Spanish-Cuban fisherman had fished here for decades. Gavino Gutierrez, the cofounder of Ybor City along with Vincente Ybor, frequently sailed down to Anna Maria Island to fish. In one of these vacations he met Casena, an elderly Spaniard who had homesteaded here for thirty-five years.

In 1894, George Emerson Bean acquired 160 acres, the island's entire northern point—the tree-lined protuberance Celi had dubbed Grove Point. The remainder of the island was dense jungle, but Bean and his son, along with a few other early settlers, cleared the brush and carved out homesites, opening the island to Northern guests. One such Northerner was Fig Newton inventor Charles Roser, who retired to Anna Maria in 1909, building a wood-frame vernacular cottage today known as Roser Cottage. Roser's wife, Caroline, died soon after arriving on Anna Maria, and he built in her memory Roser Chapel, located across the street from Roser Cottage. Roser Cottage can still be seen on Pine Avenue, near the City Pier. Roser reportedly used his earnings from his contract with Nabisco to finance the construction costs of the chapel.

Until the 1920s (and maybe thereafter—see below), Anna Maria Island visitors had to be daring. Infested with alligator, porcupine, and wild pigs, the island was accessible only by boat, with no regular ferry. Islanders needing to get to the mainland reportedly hollered across Anna Maria Sound until someone with a boat heard and retrieved them.[42] Finally, in 1922 a wooden bridge was constructed; however, it was rickety and barely wide enough to accommodate a single Model-T.[43] A drawbridge operated by hand crank, required by one account a full fifteen minutes for the passage of a single vessel. The Anna Maria Oyster Bar and fishing pier are today where the "Death Rattle" Cortez Bridge once stood.

The rickety wooden bridge was the sole means of access to Anna Maria Island until 1957, when the current steel and concrete Cortez Bridge was installed. The Cortez Bridge resulted in an explosion of interest in Anna Maria Island as day-trippers, retirees, and families sought solace and serenity on its turquoise shores.

In the 1950s, Bradenton Beach and Holmes Beach were incorporated as separate towns. Then in 1970, the island's first—*and last*—high-rise was constructed. Nothing short of violence was done to gentle Anna Maria's casual feel with the installation of the seven-story "condo killer" Martinique North Condominium. Shortly thereafter, all three towns passed ordinances limiting the height of structures to thirty-seven feet, or three stories.[44] The conscious absence of chain hotels, condominiums, and other unsightly "view killers" rendered Anna Maria soft and sweet. Today she is dotted with pastel cottages and bungalows, white picket fences and thatch huts, gently rustling palm trees, sea grapes, and sugary white dunes. For those in the know, an electric golf cart is *the* way to get around; conventional motor vehicles feel oppressive of her quiet contours and sandy niches.

22
CORTEZ FISHING VILLAGE

Crossing the Cortez Bridge to the mainland brings visitors to Cortez, Florida's last working fishing village by some reports. (I'd wager Cedar Key vies for that designation, though there tourism may have replaced fish as the chief local industry.) "The Kitchen" is what old-timers called the rich waters surrounding Cortez Fishing Village: their descendants have effortlessly drawn pompano, sea trout, mullet, and grouper from these shores for over a century, with no sign of retirement in sight by the current generation.

Cortez Fishing Village is listed on the National Register of Historic Places as a historic district.[45] Bound by Cortez Boulevard to its north and the harbor to its south, the historic district was owned by just one or two families at the turn of the twentieth century. The twenty-five acres were subsequently divided into smaller parcels, but most were sold only within the families. Cortez was planned on a grid system with no standard building setbacks. Therefore, residences and commercial buildings typically come right up to the narrow streets, without a sidewalk or yard to separate the public from the private sphere. Residential lots were also working yards where fisherfolk mended nets, iced fish, repaired vessels, and restored sails. Dwellings doubled as workshops and fishing shacks or icehouses—and still do in many cases. Nearly all houses are wood frame with clapboard siding and gabled roofs; most are one-story, but a few have two levels.

Down by the harbor are fishing shacks and net houses, also filed with the National Register. The former is defined as a wooden house built with

Residents of Florida's last working fishing village, Cortez, have mined the rich waters of Sarasota Bay continuously since the 1880s. *State Archives of Florida.*

a dock on its water side, a breezeway on the street side. In its central area, fishermen processed fish for market. Off the center working area was an office to one side and an icehouse to the other. The fish shack also functioned as a "town square," where local men would meet, discuss the forecast, hear news, and exchange stories. One historic fishing shack remains in the district: the Fulford Fish House (1940) off 123rd Street West, next to the Star Fish Company. The Star Fish and A.P. Bell are the two chief fish markets in Cortez today.

Net camps are small, low buildings constructed directly on the dock or stilted offshore in the harbor, several of which are still extant. The Johns-Capo Net Camp (1935) is located south of the Star Fish about two hundred yards offshore and is wood-frame with a wrap-around porch and a net-spread, a cluster of wooden pilings placed so as to hold a newly woven net suspended over the water to dry in the sun.

Though the people of Cortez have always shared a similar vision of fishing for one's life and livelihood, a controversy sprang up in the 1920s concerning net-making. The conflict arose from the size of holes in the nets: traditionally, a gillnet was used, named so because the gills would snag on the netting as the fish tried to escape. The gillnet was historically preferred because it captured only a specific size of fish. In the 1920s, some fishermen began using a stopnet, which caught every size and type of fish, causing waste and destruction of the resource. The conflict culminated in the dynamiting of the home of local gillnetter Joe Fulford, whose descendants today run the A.P. Bell Fish Company next to the Star Fish. The home was only partly damaged, and today it is a private residence.

A few public buildings served the people of Cortez, beginning with a one-room schoolhouse built in 1896. Pine was hauled by oxcart eight miles from a mill in Palma Sola for its construction. The school is now located on 45th Avenue West and is a private residence. A new school was constructed in 1912, the first brick school in Manatee County. The Cortez Rural Graded School enrolled children grades one through eight in two large rooms and operated until 1961, when it was sold to an art school. Today, the original 1912 brick building is home to the Florida Maritime Museum. Finally, the tabby-wall jail was constructed in 1931, though it reportedly served only one occupant (and his wife helped him escape the same night of his jailing, though to her credit she obtained permission from authorities before bringing him home). The sole occupant was arrested for drinking and rowdiness; thereafter, the long arm of the law didn't find occasion to reach into the quiet, industrious fishing town of Cortez. The tabby jail still stands today on private property off 124th Street Court West and serves as the property owner's laundry house.

The Star Fish Company seafood market on the southern shore of the peninsula redefines "fresh seafood." Inside, the morning's catch is displayed behind polished glass, gleaming atop piles of ice from stainless-steel trays. Out back, mismatched umbrellas shade packed dockside picnic tables seating a mishmash crowd of snowbirds, fishermen, and locals enjoying crab salad, raw oysters, fried clams, shrimp, and cod. The February or March lunch rush can snake around the building—if it can be called that—more of a fishing shack, icehouse, and tumbledown marina, all wrapped up into one. Order at the tiny window when it's your turn; duck to be heard by the lady at the register. An icy Corona in hand, make your way to the seat-yourself dining area, and maybe you'll be lucky enough to snag a spot among the pelicans and the patrons to wait for your food. If not, find a vacant wooden piling, use its round top as a tiny stand for your beer, and relax—no one will mind.

In the twenty-first century, the Cortez Fishing Village lives on as a "place where ordinary people doing ordinary things have worked and prayed together in a perhaps ordinary way to create a way of life that today seems extraordinary."[46]

23

GAMBLE PLANTATION AND A NARROW CONFEDERATE ESCAPE

En route to Snead Island near Anna Maria, visitors traveling from I-75 may notice a curiosity on the right side of US 301: a stately antebellum mansion with Neoclassical white columns and a handsome pediment (the triangular gable atop the columns in the Greco-Roman style of architecture). An immense green lawn stretches before the residence, with a few outbuildings and smaller structures dotting the landscape.

Around 1840, Major Robert Gamble started a sugar plantation here near the historic town of Manatee, on the banks of the Manatee River.[47] Though today US-301 separates the 13-acre historic site from the Manatee River on its south side, when Major Gamble built the house, his property lay directly on the waterway. Gamble's plantation was a success: at one point, 200 workers, mainly enslaved laborers, worked 3,500 acres, producing by one account 1,500 hogsheads of sugar per year, the equivalent of over 485,000 pounds. (One hogshead barrel held about 330 pounds of sugar; a hogshead was a British unit of measurement related to the standard wooden barrel used to transport large quantities of liquid, like cider or wine, or solids like tobacco or sugar.)

By the time of the Civil War, all of Manatee County had backed the Confederacy, including the then-occupant of Gamble Plantation, Captain Archibald McNeil. At that time, Captain McNeil provided about two-thirds of his annual sugar crop to the Rebel commissary. Unfortunately for McNeil, this caught the attention of the Union forces: a federal steamship sailed quietly up the dark Manatee River under cover of night, disembarked at McNeil's plantation, and proceeded to dynamite the Confederate sympathizer's sugar mill. The ruins of the tabby sugar mill are extant about half a mile north of Gamble Plantation and can be viewed from Ellenton-Gillette Road, on the east side of the road.

The Gamble estate played a key role in the "mythical escape" of a Confederate official named Judah Philip Benjamin, the secretary of state of the Confederacy under Jefferson Davis. The story has been told many times, and its hero, Judah P. Benjamin, has taken on the aura of a kind of folk hero, for better or for worse.[48]

It was the late spring of 1865. Things were not looking good for the Southern Cause. The Confederate Cabinet had just adjourned its final meeting in Georgia and was already on the run, having just received notice that U.S. Federal troops were closing in. Benjamin was well known to the Union: He not only held an important cabinet position but also was

Major Robert Gamble began this antebellum mansion in 1840, but its most famous occupant was Judah P. Benjamin, a colorful Confederate outlaw who hid in the woodpile behind the mansion to escape detection by Union forces. *"Gamble Plantation Historic State Park" by Ebyabe CC BY-SA 3.0.*

informally considered the "brains behind the Confederacy." He was also the first Jewish person to hold an office of any kind in the U.S. government. (Benjamin was a cousin of David Levy Yulee, for whom Levy County near Cedar Key is named.)

Being a longtime resident of New Orleans, Benjamin naturally fled south into the swamplands of southern Georgia. By one account, he disguised himself as a Frenchman called Monsieur Bonfals, French-Cajun for "a good disguise" (Benjamin seems to have kept his sense of humor—and his wits about him—throughout his escape.) On May 3, 1865, Benjamin found himself in Northern Florida near present-day Gainesville. A kindhearted farmer's wife made him a poor laborer's suit with which to travel through Florida, and he secured the oldest, worst horse and buggy he could find as transportation. At some point, he heard a tale of an unassuming sugar plantation in the backwoods along the Manatee River. Wanting to avoid population centers, Benjamin found his way to Gamble Plantation. The McNeil family sheltered Benjamin for ten days, at one point hiding him in a woodpile due to a raid of Union troops looking for the fugitive.

Next, Benjamin was transported to the home of another Manatee County resident living about one and one-half miles south of the McNeil's estate. A former slave drove the oxcart that held Benjamin, covered in freshly butchered meat and palmetto leaves. In the dead of night, Benjamin, by that time likely of pungent odor, exited his oxcart at the home of William Whitaker, who is credited with the first marriage and fathering the first white child in Sarasota.[49] Present-day Whitaker Gateway Park, Whitaker Bayou, and Whitaker Lane all call William Whitaker their namesake. This area sits west of US-41, just north of the intersection with Fruitville Avenue.

On June 23, after a month of hiding out near Sarasota Bay, likely on or around Whitaker's homestead, Benjamin boarded the *Blonde*, a small sloop secured by another Confederate sympathizer, Captain Tesca. The *Blonde* quietly sailed south, dodging Union blockade vessels, which were very active in Florida's west coast at the close of the war, when many Confederate players sought escape from prosecution. By this time, the Union had publicly offered a $25,000 reward for the body of Judah P Benjamin—dead or alive.

Near Gasparilla Island, Union officials boarded the *Blonde*, scarching for Confederate escapees, including Benjamin. Always his wits about him, Benjamin donned a cook's apron, bathed his hands and face in cooking grease, and stood in the galley, hiding in plain sight of the raiding officials. One of the Federal troops is rumored to have remarked that he'd "never seen a Jewish cook before."[50]

Judah P. Benjamin arrived in the Bahamas on July 10, where he boarded a British steamer, and on August 30, he arrived safely in Southampton. Benjamin took up residence in England and successfully practiced law there for many more years, involving himself in several high-profile cases in London.

From his initial flight after the last cabinet meeting in Georgia to the waiting British steamer in the Bahamas and all the way to Europe, not one solitary player in the lengthy escape saga ever told the Union government where Benjamin was hiding or shared details leading to his capture.[51]

In the 1930s, under threat of demolition, Gamble Plantation was acquired by the Manatee Chapter of the Daughters of the Confederacy, which still owns and maintains the antebellum mansion to this day. A Confederate memorial to Judah P. Benjamin is located on site.

24
ANGOLA SLAVE COLONY AND BRADEN CASTLE

Bradenton (formerly spelled *Braiden-town*) sits on the Manatee River, about eight miles from its mouth at Tampa Bay. Wares Creek, near the bridge just east of the Bradenton Women's Club, was the original western boundary of the nascent town of Braden and still marks the western boundary of downtown Bradenton. Bradenton's first settler was Josiah Gates, who in 1843 built a log home at the present-day location of Manatee Mineral Springs Park.[52]

Prior to Gates's arrival, a tiny colony of maroons (escaped Black slaves) thrived here in the 1820s. This settlement, called by historians the Angola Escaped Slave Colony, was composed mainly of escapees from Alabama, Georgia, and South Carolina who supported themselves by light farming and fishing the Manatee River's rich waters; an on-site spring provided fresh drinking water.[53] After only a single decade of successful yet simple existence here, the colony was raided by federal troops who burned the rustic structures and captured most of the residents, including men, women, and children. Some of the Angola residents were able to escape to Key Biscayne and then to the Bahamas, likely with the help of allies in the Seminole tribe.

The county's only natural spring, Manatee Mineral Spring, attracted both the Angola colonists and the earliest settlers. Gates's choice was almost certainly based on the proximity of the spring, which still bubbles feebly on this spot. A nascent village arose nearby around 1850, just northeast of the present-day Manatee Village Historic Park. The original

Manatee County Courthouse (1860–66), which has been moved to the park, functioned when the Gates family homesteaded here. The grave marker of Josiah Gates (1802–1871) can still be seen at the cemetery across the street; the original courthouse square was a block farther. This little wood-frame vernacular structure was the center of law and justice for all of vast Manatee County (1850), which originally stretched from the Manatee River south to the Caloosahatchee River (Fort Myers) and east to Lake Okeechobee. In 1866, the county seat was moved to Pine Level in Arcadia; it reverted to the Bradenton area in 1887 when DeSoto County was carved from Manatee, thus removing Pine Level from Manatee County's jurisdiction. The current Manatee County Courthouse was constructed in 1913 and is located a mile west of the village of Manatee in downtown Bradenton.

In 1842, another early settler, and Bradenton's namesake, Joseph Braden, arrived here from Virginia after a short stop in Tallahassee. Braden, like the founder of the Gamble Plantation across the Manatee River, lost his Tallahassee plantation in the National Panic of 1837, in which many new settlers surrendered their heavily mortgaged properties to foreclosing banks. Both Braden and Gamble headed south and started over on new sugar plantations on the banks of the semitropical Manatee River.

During his time on the Manatee River, approximately 1848 to 1856, Braden constructed a unique residence, a kind of miniature tabby fortress, the ruins of which can still be seen where Braden River joins the Manatee River, today known as the Braden Castle Historic District.[54] In 1856, famed Seminole Chief Billy Bowlegs attacked Braden's residence. He made off with many of Braden's slaves, who mostly lived in thatched huts and other crude housing near the fortress–main residence. The braves plundered Braden's outbuildings and destroyed most of his sugarworks. A subsequent account by Braden's neighbor Gamble relates that Bowlegs's band had lurked around the castle, quietly "casing the joint" by night, before finally launching an attack.[55] All of Braden's household survived, and his (apparently aptly designed) castle sustained no major damage, being constructed entirely of stone. Shortly after the Indian attack, yet another financial panic caused Braden's current mortgage holder to foreclose, at which point Braden moved to Texas, where he died in 1888.

Although Braden Castle Historic District's name[56] invokes its founder, much of its "history" dates from the 1920s and 1930s, during the age of "tin-can tourism." This phenomenon refers to the influx of Northerners in motorcars who traveled to Florida in huge numbers during the Great

Depression for vacation or seeking a new life away from their troubles in depressed (and frigid!) Northern cities. Their emblem featured a small can of soup atop a car radiator, an image designed to embrace members' thriftiness, resourcefulness, and, of course, penchant for motor travel. Bradenton Beach, near the old wooden bridge to Cortez Fishing Village, was also a destination of these Depression-era travelers, who famously made lemons into lemonade. (An interesting spit of land farther south near Pine Island in Charlotte County, today known as Matlache, also harbored tin-can tourists during the Great Depression.) Though some wealthier Floridians disliked the tin-can crowd, many others welcomed the blue-collar newcomer with his wholesome, endearing sense of humor in the face of often crippling trial.

In 1924, the Camping Tourists of America, the tin-canners' national organization (CTC), purchased the Braden Castle tract, at that time a neglected orange grove. The new owners subdivided the parcel into intentionally tiny lots (thirty-seven feet by thirty-seven feet) and by 1929 had constructed over 180 tiny residences. Most were torn down in the 1970s for the installation of mobile homes, but a few were merely updated: For example, the tiny Mediterranean Revival at 46 Braden Castle Drive across the road from the castle ruins. The tiny lots left ample common areas for shuffleboard, lawn games, and pavilions, as well as public bathing houses and laundry facilities.

It is worth noting that a century later, a new RV and "tiny house" culture soared in popularity in the face of inflation and overall malaise of great Northern cities during and after the COVID-19 pandemic. The two phenomena, the tin-can tourists of the 1920s and the RV and tiny-housers of the 2020s in many ways represent what's still great about America: thrift, optimism, and resilience in the face of trial.

25

MABLE RINGLING'S ROSE GARDEN

C*à d'Zan* roughly translates to "House of John," but the property today known as the Ringling Estate in Sarasota was the pride and joy of his wife, Mable. Although Mable Ringling died only three years after the completion of her masterpiece, the Venetian home with its meticulously selected interior furnishings and décor, and especially the Rose Garden, exude Mrs. Ringling's superb taste, gracious style, and timeless beauty. In their will, the Ringlings bequeathed the entire property to the State of Florida and expressed a wish that it become a Venetian art museum for the next generation of Floridians. Though the state attempted to carry out the Ringlings' last wish, the public expressed a desire for more of Mrs. Ringling rather than an exotic and foreign art gallery. As a result, the focus of the Ringling Estate has always been about the home of the circus man and his intriguing bride, the art collection playing second fiddle in the public eye.[57]

Mable Ringling was born Armilda Burton on March 14, 1875, in Moon, Ohio, and was one of six children. Reticent by nature, Mrs. Ringling revealed little of her personal history during her relatively short life. It might be said that she expressed herself in her contributions to art, architecture, and landscape rather than words. We do know that by 1900 she'd moved to New York to find gainful employment, suggesting that her family was one of limited means. Mable's family ties were strong: her many siblings visited her Sarasota winter home frequently, and several bought land nearby.[58]

Soon after her arrival in the Northeast, she met her husband, circus magnate John Ringling, and the two were married in Hoboken, New Jersey, in 1905. Mrs. Ringling first took an interest in the Sarasota area in 1911, when she and John began wintering here. That same year, they bought the twenty-acre property on Sarasota Bay from Charles Thompson, the developer of Shell Beach Subdivision and also a circus man. On site was a twelve-room wood-frame structure known as Palms Elysian. (This name draws on Greek mythology, Elysium Fields of the underworld being where the most virtuous or heroic souls reside after death.)

Even before construction began on the Cà d'Zan, Mable planned her beloved rose garden. Indeed, the layout of the thirty-room Italianate mansion seems to complement the formal rose garden, rather than the other way around. When later planning the Cà d'Zan, Mable selected an east-facing room for her personal quarters, with a garden view, rather than a bay view. Mrs. Ringling drew from her travels in Venice when planning the layout for the garden's Italianate wagon wheel beds, radiating from a central stone gazebo crowned with a wrought-iron dome.

Italianate architecture differs from that of an Italian villa, in that the former uses geometric shapes and tends to be less fluid and curved. The Italianate rose garden's balance and symmetry exemplify this high structure and formality.[59] (Compare the rigid structure of Mable's wagon wheel design and geometric beds to a meandering garden walk among round or irregular beds, curving organically over a bucolic stream; the latter would fit the Italian villa, though not the Italianate style.) Yet to soften the structure of the landscape, statuary of Italian peasant couples in courtship gestures and poses lend an air of romance to the space. Its center gazebo of stone and wrought iron would have invited Mable's guests at her garden parties and lawn socials to rest awhile and enjoy the well-ordered and meticulously planned greenspace. *Gazebo* derives from the English word *gaze*; its ending might arise from a tongue-in-cheek reference to Latin future tense ending *-abo*: this would result in the structure's literal name being "I will gaze."[60]

The garden's backdrop is a magnificent banyan wood, originating in thirteen banyan trees gifted from Thomas Edison's estate in Fort Myers. Sarasota boasts several notable banyan trees, including the ones at Maria Selby Gardens and Historic Spanish Point. All these banyans (the Ringlings' included) are said to be sourced from a single four-foot sapling shipped to Edison in a butter tub from India for his botanical laboratory in Fort Myers.[61]

The John Ringling Estate on Sarasota Bay was planned so Mable Ringling could view her Italianate rose garden from her bedroom window. Sculptures of Venetian peasants soften the geometric regularity of the garden's perfectly symmetrical beds. *Courtesy of the Sarasota Rose Society.*

Mable Ringling died in 1929, just three years after the completion of Cà d'Zan. The estate fell into disrepair after the Great Depression but was later revived by the State of Florida. On-site horticulturalist Ron Mallory developed the Mable Ringling Rose in 2001, registered with the American Rose Society: a fiery red rose with a hint of yellow and a mellow, sensual fragrance.[62]

Today the Ringling Estate encompasses the magnificent art collection, including a replica of the statue of *David*, which has also become the City of Sarasota's emblem. The estate also includes the garden and grounds, a modern Circus Museum, a playground, the now-immense banyan wood, and several cozy cafés, as well as a state-of-the-art Museum Welcome Center and Gift Shop.

26

PINECRAFT VILLAGE

FLORIDA'S ONLY OLD-ORDER SETTLEMENT

In 1923, a group of elderly Amish traveled to Florida to escape the cold and seek a healthier climate. From the heart to the sinuses, Florida's mild winters were said to cure the body and renew the mind and heart. Sarasota quickly became a winter destination for Amish and Mennonites of all varieties, and Bahia Vista, an unassuming connector of US-41 and Cattlemen Road, has become the unofficial "Main Street" of Amish culture in Florida.

This area of Sarasota—beginning at the intersection of Bahia Vista Street and South Beneva Road and sprawling several city blocks in each direction—is now known as Pinecraft. From November to April, it is a bustling hub of activity for Amish and Mennonites.

Yoder's Amish Village is a restaurant, a gift shop, and a farm market, all sharing a tiny parking lot often completely packed at lunchtime in February and March. Look for the line of people snaking around the small restaurant building toward the back parking lot, with wait times often exceeding an hour. Lunch guests are relieved to graduate from the alley to the breezeway and then again when they actually enter the indoor waiting area, perhaps lucky enough to snag a seat on a bench. A stone's throw from the restaurant is a gift shop selling Amish crafts and home décor and a farm market with jellies, prepared foods, and baked goods. The three businesses that make up Yoder's Amish Village all share a parking lot and occupy approximately half a city block in the heart of Pinecraft. Across Bahia Vista and diagonal from the Yoder's compound is Der Dutchman, a family-style buffet restaurant, larger, less traditional than Yoder's and better suited to groups.

Also of note in this area are Miller's Dutch Haus Furniture and Alma Sue's Quilt Shop, both located in the no-frills plaza adjacent to Der Dutchman. The quilt shop boasts gorgeous, authentic Amish handmade quilts and coverlets of every color of the rainbow, ranging from $1,200 to $1,600 depending on the intricacy of the design and materials.

Running north–south behind this plaza is the Legacy Trail, an eighteen-and-a-half-mile biking, skating, and foot trail beginning at the Historic Venice Train Depot in downtown Venice and tracing the historic route of the Seaboard Airline Railway, which can still be seen on some stretches of the paved recreational use trail. Because of their limited means of transportation, Old Order communities have especially benefited from the Legacy Trail's completion in 2022.

The bike path connecting thirty-two access points across the urban core of Sarasota allows the Amish (and others) to move about safely and easily, and it has contributed to the increase in winter visitors from Old Order communities of every stripe.

Southward on Bahia Vista is Pinecraft Park on the shores of Philippi Creek, which snakes its way the length of Sarasota from the interior of Myakka until it empties into Sarasota Bay near Phillippi Estate Park. Pinecraft Park is the unofficial daytime meeting spot for Mennonite senior

Upward of $1,600 is what prospective buyers can expect to pay for a handsewn queen-size Amish quilt in Sarasota's Pinecraft village. Amish quilters, bakers, and artisans arrived in rural Sarasota at the turn of the twentieth century, and their descendants continue to winter near Siesta Key to the present day. *Author photo.*

citizens, who ride their bicycles or tricycles from the village and congregate on mild winter afternoons for shuffleboard and news. Shuffleboard, generally frowned upon by the more conservative sects of the Old Order Amish up north, is a favorite pastime for those who might not engage in such frivolity back home.

Pinecraft is marked with rows of neat, immaculately kept yards and dwellings, and the quaint street names represent old Amish and Mennonite families: Kruppa, Graber, and Miller Avenues. These road names attest to the longevity of Old Order winter homes in this area. Most Pinecraft homes have been held by the same family since the Amish began vacationing here in the 1920s. These small, neat vacation cottages rarely change hands; most families keep the properties for winter vacationing of extended relatives and church members and rent the properties to other Amish or Mennonite in the off-season.

Many Old Order families elected to make Sarasota their year-round home, so the community now includes schools and permanent churches. Mennonite children can often be seen in the yard of the small white schoolhouse off Honore Avenue, just past the sign for Sunnyside Mennonite Church.

East of Pinecraft, where Palmer Boulevard intersects Cattleman Road, is the original Detwiler's Farm Market, now a household name for locals, offering fresh produce, groceries, Amish-rolled butter, meats, cheeses, pies, baked goods, and ice cream at affordable prices. The Detwiler family opened the market in the early 2000s, further evidencing the influence and the permanence of Amish and Mennonite culture in the Sarasota area. Not just quilts and butter anymore, the Detwiler's chain of stores has now spread north to Palmetto and south to Venice, with a half-dozen total locations, providing significant localized competition to Lakeland, Florida–based Publix Supermarkets, the gold-standard of Florida supermarket shopping.

A mile east of Detwiler's, lies the Celery Fields, bisected by Palmer. The four-hundred-acre bird sanctuary is currently maintained by the Audubon Society. The Amish were initially drawn to this area hoping to engage in their normal career of choice, farming, and the fields around the acreage now known as the "Celery Fields" were marketed as tillable. Mrs. Potter (Bertha) Palmer, for whom this road is named, initiated the project to drain the marsh and transform it into farmland for a variety of vegetables back in 1923, about the time the Amish were arriving. It was soon discovered that celery especially flourished here, and the Amish began farming the area in earnest, until it was acquired by the county in 1995. Present-day Celery Fields is a suburban nature park, but prior to the 1990s, this area of Palmer Avenue was extremely remote, Pinecraft Village being the extreme outer reaches of the town of Sarasota.

The giant green hill or mound in the center of the preserve was a result of excavating the surrounding lakes and canals, which was necessary to make the area farmable since it was marshy slough back in the 1920s and 1930s when this work was initially conceived by Bertha Palmer (she died in 1918, but others took up her effort in subsequent years).

The Sarasota Audubon Society now runs and administers the wetlands, and the area has become a favorite of birders and bird photographers from all over the state, attracting 250 bird species, from the American bald eagle to the roseate spoonbill and the purple martin. Sandhill cranes and white pelicans are especially common in this area. The Nature Center, located at a turnoff at the bottom of the hill just before Center Road, is open October through May on weekdays 9:00 a.m. to noon and until 3:00 p.m. on weekends.

Celery Fields, and its evolution from slough and marshland to successful, productive celery fields, back to bird sanctuary, again attests to the influence the Amish have had in the Sarasota area. One wonders, if these "transplants" from the North hadn't so diligently farmed this area from the early 1920s to the 1990s, would Celery Fields, Pinecraft, and East Sarasota have become the bustling neighborhoods they are today?

27

SARASOTA'S LEADING LADY

BERTHA PALMER'S HOMESTEAD

Sarasota's leading lady, the *exceptional* Bertha Honore Palmer, was born Bertha Matilda Honore in 1849 in Kentucky, one of six children.[63] Her maternal grandmother, though steeped deeply in Southern culture, freed her slaves far prior to the Emancipation Proclamation due to personal scruples. This social conscientiousness and relative progressivism, combined with reverence for human dignity, affected the lifework of her remarkable granddaughter.[64]

When Bertha was six, the Honore family moved to Chicago, at that time a dusty up-and-coming city of about forty thousand. Her father was a developer and invested in land, which he subdivided and sold to other wealthy Southern families moving to the big city.

Miss Honore was not only accomplished, intelligent, and beautiful but also a woman of the highest character: her strict adherence to truth, no matter the cost, carried throughout her life.[65] High principles and gracious manners shaped Bertha's youth, womanhood, marriage, and later, when Florida captured her attention, widowhood.

OSPREY POINT, AS IT WAS WHEN SHE FOUND IT

Meanwhile, in 1867, pioneers John and Eliza Webb of Utica, New York, heard tell of the wholesome climate of La Florida, still a young state, having joined the Union only twenty-two years prior in 1845.[66] A trader in Key West told John of a high point on the western coast of Florida, perhaps the perfect site for their hopeful new beginning: homesteading and raising citrus to send up north. The slight elevation of this "high point" offers natural protection from the coastal flooding and the mangrove estuary environment characterizing the otherwise low-lying shoreline of Sarasota Bay; as a result, the Webbs' homestead flourished. Today, the Webb compound, known as Selby Gardens-Historic Spanish Point Campus, is maintained by Selby Gardens.

Extant Webb family properties include a nineteenth-century white clapboard farmhouse, a boatyard, and Cock's Footbridge, a wooden walkway across the mangrove estuary. The farmhouse belonged to Webb's son-in-law, who worked as a boatwright here. Farther south, directly on the seashore is the Webb packinghouse, where the Webb family shipped its citrus fruit south to Key West, around the tip of Florida, then up the Eastern Seaboard, back to their native New York. (Selby Gardens furnishes the packinghouse with the crates and chutes the citrus growers used to size and sort the fruit, as well as plastic fruit to try out the chutes.) A dock leads out into crystal-clear blue Sarasota Bay, and the turquoise water is a striking backdrop against the natural wood packinghouse and bright orange fruit replicas.

Mary's Chapel lies at the end of a quick walk through a shelled forest path from the packinghouse. Mary's Chapel is a beautifully restored wooden pioneer church of the vernacular style and was fitted with stained-glass windows in a renovation in the mid-1980s. The original structure was built by the parents of a young girl who visited the Webb family from the North, hoping the highly prized warm climate and wholesome sea air would restore her health. The "Fountain of Youth" myth of warm, healing springs and wholesome, curative sea breezes encouraged many Northerners to pursue the supernatural in Florida's sultry climate.

Mary died at Spanish Point, and her mother and father built this chapel in her memory, where the entire Webb and Guptill families were eventually buried (Mary's folks buried her back North, so, ironically, hers is not among the headstones of the chapel bearing her name).

CHICAGO'S LEADING LADY

By the late 1800s, Miss Honore had become Mrs. Bertha Honore Palmer, wife of Chicago merchant Potter Palmer, a Quaker, who made his fortune as the owner of general stores in Chicago. Though now a veritable socialite who had traveled the world and "had $200,000—and that was just around her neck" (Bertha adored fine jewels), Mrs. Palmer never compromised her morals. A strong voice for the Woman's Christian Temperance Union, Mrs. Palmer firmly believed that drunkenness caused breadwinners to shirk their duties to their families, forcing women to work outside the home, leading to the decline of the family and, by extension, society.[67]

Myriad other charitable causes filled Mrs. Palmer's calendar, in addition to the education of her sons Honore ("Min" for his small stature) and Potter Jr. ("Cappy"). Bertha became interested in training ladies in fine handiwork and decorative crafting to uplift themselves and their families after the Civil War. Her interest culminated in her role as lady manager of the Chicago World's Fair women's exhibition, displaying fine arts by women. Some complained that Mrs. Palmer denied women prominence in separating them from men's exhibitions, but she was firm that keeping the women's contributions in their own sphere would illuminate the unique beauty of the feminine perspective. Mrs. Palmer always distanced herself from any faction that could be considered fringe or radical. Though often criticized by suffragists who desired her blessing—and financial support—Mrs. Palmer held firm that a woman's sphere was in making the world one of gracious beauty and goodness, not in competition with her husband, father, and brothers.

OSPREY POINT, THE OAKS, MEADOWSWEET PASTURES, PALMER RANCH

Potter Palmer, twenty-three years Bertha's senior, died in 1901, and the widowed Bertha Honore Palmer came to Florida in 1911. Her biographers note a change in Bertha during this time: her interest in world travel, fine art, and exquisite jewelry began to fade.[68] Her refuge was now among seashells, swamps, and Seminoles: she purchased nearly fifty square miles of property just in Sarasota during this last decade of her life, including the Webb homestead. The sprawling Sarasota development of Palmer Ranch takes its name from its original foundress.

She called the highpoint today known as Historic Spanish Point "Osprey Point." She also purchased a home on the adjacent tract from Laurence Jones of the Four Roses bourbon dynasty, naming this estate The Oaks. The Oaks evolved into the exclusive Oaks subdivision in Sarasota, a bayside residential development offering exclusive properties to Sarasota's most discriminating buyers. She called the white clapboard farmhouse previously belonging to Guptill "Hill House."

Not everyone in Florida was pleased about its new benefactress. Local Ku Klux Klan members were openly annoyed at the activity of Palmer in Sarasota at this time: She was not only a carpetbagger but also a well-educated woman with an agenda of her own, which the Klansmen could not understand. Moreover, she cared about the poor, especially poor women, Black or white.

An incident involving an accusation that one of Palmer's boarder-employees had stolen a hog from a neighboring property illuminates the ferocity of her devotion to the welfare of her hired hands. When the accusation prompted the local sheriff to enter Bertha Palmer's property unannounced, the socialite turned rancher was livid: "One of my negroes' quarters was searched which took most of the afternoon," she later wrote to her lawyer. "What formalities is the sheriff obliged to comply with? Should he not be forced to come to me or my superintendent and show his warrant and have assent to search the quarters?"[69]

Palmer also acquired thousands of acres of what is today Myakka River State Park, which she used as a ranch and dubbed Meadowsweet Pastures. Her sons granted a large tract of Meadowsweet Pastures to the State of Florida after her death, which was the inception of the state park. From her headquarters at the "Home Farm" (what is today the Oaks subdivision), Palmer was involved in every aspect of the ranching operations underway at Meadowsweet, ten miles east–northeast from her central command. At one point, she employed over three hundred workers on her properties, many of them African Americans who boarded at Osprey Point. The arrival of Mrs. Palmer virtually put an end to joblessness in Manatee County (Sarasota County wasn't created out of Manatee's boundaries until 1921).

Sadly, Bertha Palmer, renowned for her health and vitality, met her match with a fatal breast cancer diagnosis in 1917. Despite a mastectomy from the best surgeons in New York the same year, she was told the unthinkable: She had only a short time to live. Palmer succumbed to cancer on May 5, 1918, only four months after berating her lawyer for the behavior of the sheriff deputy on her land in the hog thief incident (see previous page). She remained fully involved in her ranching operations, the welfare of her employees and farmhands, the farming practices at Meadowsweet Pastures, and the maintenance of her beloved Oaks, until nearly her final hour.

Bertha Palmer was responsible for the naming and mapping of Honore Avenue, Palmer Avenue, Tuttle Avenue, Lockwood Ridge Road, and Macintosh Road, all key arteries in Sarasota to this day. The Oaks, Historic Spanish Point, Palmer Ranch, Potters Park, Celery Fields, and Myakka River State Park owe their status to Palmer and her descendants.[70] It's no wonder Sarasota, the grateful former frontier town with a population of four hundred, preserved these commemorative tributes to its founding mother.

28

OLD MIAKKA'S CROWLEY MUSEUM AND THE ROAD TO PINE LEVEL

The unincorporated community of Old Miakka east of Sarasota was originally settled in the 1850s by Florida Cracker cow hunters. *Cracker* is a word you'll hear often when exploring the backroads and byways of Florida. This was originally a nickname for Florida "cow hunters" who ranged their cattle on unfenced land, paying little attention to their stock until the fall roundup. (But don't call them cowboys—those are in Texas!) Crackers used twelve-to-fifteen-foot bullwhips, which they snapped loudly a few inches from a cow's ear to drive it to the cattle docks at Fort Myers, Punta Rassa, Burnt Store, or Punta Gorda for shipment to New Orleans, Key West, Fort Brooke (Tampa), or even Cuba. The crack of these whips rang out like gunshots over the prairies and swamps, thus the cow hunters came to be called "crackers."[71] Cracker is now a term for any Florida native who resides, or whose ancestors resided, in a rural area.

Old Miakka differs from nearby Myakka City in more than just its spelling, the latter being a bit of a tender subject for Miakka locals. As the local legend goes, the fellow who registered Old Miakka for a post office with the federal government had such poor handwriting that the community was permanently enrolled as Myakka.[72] Much later in 1915, when Myakka City was incorporated (actually about ten miles northeast of the original Old Miakka), its purpose was to accommodate a whistlestop depot of the East West Railway. The (incorrect) spelling was used because Old Miakka, the unincorporated community that had flourished for over half of a century, appeared under the incorrect spelling ("Old Myakka") on federal documents.

Off Miakka Road at the junction with Wilson Road in eastern Sarasota County is Old Miakka Schoolhouse (1914) listed on the National Register of Historic Places. Farther down Miakka Road past the still-active Old Miakka United Methodist Church (1886) is the Crowley Museum and Nature Center entrance on the east side of the road.

The collection of pioneer buildings assembled in this 191-acre living museum represents several generations of two pioneering families, the Crowleys and the Tatums. The collection of historic buildings could occupy an entire afternoon, but a few monuments and structures are especially worthwhile.

One of the finest examples of a historic dwelling at the Museum, and arguably in Sarasota County, is the Tatum House. This two-story clapboard wooden structure was moved from its original location at the corner of Proctor and Interstate 75, behind today's Sarasota Baptist Church. Pioneer William Harvey Tatum built the house in 1890 for his wife, Laura Fedonia Redd Rawls, and their eventual thirteen children. Laura's family, the Redds, were the original settlers on Bee Ridge, which refers to the area between Clark and Fruitville Roads today, the western boundary being Philippe Creek and eastern boundary Cowpen Slough. Its name is based on its high and dry situation at around fourteen feet above sea level and the prevalence of wild honeybees found there.

Where the designated boardwalk ends and the trail returns to soft ground, an overgrown trail leads to the original circa 1870s wooden sign marking Cowpath Lane, covered in brambles and vines. Following Cowpath about ten minutes deeper into the woods reveals an untouched one-room cottage that brings to mind Hansel and Gretel or the seven dwarves. The aspect most prominently exposes the original brick fireplace and chimney, nearly obscured by a century of overgrowth. No sign marks the Cowpath unnamed cottage, and its ownership and origin are unclear, but it's worth the trek in the trees along the pioneer cattle trail to experience, unfiltered, what Jasper Crowley might have seen as he returned after a long day hunting cattle or boar in the surrounding woods.

Also located on site at the Crowley Museum is a portion of the original road to Pine Level, the county seat of Manatee County from 1866 to 1887. Recall that at this time, Manatee County encompassed a huge swath of land that today includes Manatee, Sarasota, Charlotte, Lee, Glades, Hendry, DeSoto, Hardee, and Highlands Counties. The original county seat was the village of Manatee, where the original wooden courthouse is still standing near the old courthouse square, today the Manatee Village Historical Park.

The county seat was moved to Pine Level in 1866 because of complaints that the Manatee Village location on the county's northern outskirts poorly served citizens residing in more southern portions. Pine Level seems to have been selected by the county fathers only because of its location in the precise center of the original Manatee County boundaries. A small town quickly came into being, as Manatee County residents from Braiden-town to Punta Gorda trudged through the swamp and the sloughs to the county seat to file claims, record plats and deeds, and conduct county business.[73]

An incident from the founding of Punta Gorda, about thirty miles south of Old Miakka on the other side of the original jurisdiction of Manatee County, demonstrates the role of the now-ghost town of Pine Level in Florida's frontier.

Sarasota pioneer William Harvey Tatum hand built this splendid A-frame wooden house near present-day Proctor Avenue in Sarasota; it was moved from its original location to the Old Miakka historical park in 1996. *Author photo.*

Back in 1884, Colonel Trabue and his wife, natives of Kentucky, purchased thirty acres of property sight unseen where Punta Gorda lies today and decided to start a town bearing his name. The City of Trabue was on the books for incorporation when Trabue's hired surveyor, a man by the name of Kelly Harvey, decided he liked the area so much he wanted a part in its founding. The local folks had not been overly impressed with the Kentucky colonel's vision for their community and, after a dispute over the funding of drainage ditches and sidewalks, joined forces with Harvey. A group of twenty or so local men gathered one warm December evening at a local pool hall on the second floor of a drugstore and voted on the town name of Punta Gorda, or "Fat Point," according to what the old Spanish maps had always called the area. The coterie of twenty-one men, including four African Americans, walked that very night thirty miles to Pine Level to file the articles of incorporation of the town "Punta Gorda." Thus the City of Punta Gorda was born. Colonel Trabue later reminisced that the people of the town stole it right out from under his handlebar mustache.[74]

The distance of Pine Level from, well, just about anywhere in Florida in the late 1800s, became legendary. To do business in Florida, you had to walk through swamps and over soft and sandy paths infested with alligators and mosquitoes. The county sheriff, jail, and courthouse were here, leaving most of Manatee County's vast reaches to vigilantes, volunteers, and citizen arrests. The road to Pine Level from Braiden-town became a well-worn thoroughfare over the two decades of its location as the Manatee County seat. "The Road to Pine Level" original route bisects Crowley Nature Center, and visitors may trample the trek of the earliest settlers. The rush to Pine Level for Florida's founders—and the often high-stakes competition among claimants over who could best navigate the difficult terrain and arrive first to record the deed—cemented Florida's reputation as a lawless Wild West in the 1880s.

29

ROOSEVELT'S TREE ARMY TAMES WILD MIAKKA

Myakka River State Park was yet another project initiated by Bertha Palmer, who purchased the area along with the rest of the land east of Sarasota in the early 1900s. It was originally a swine and cattle ranch but fell into disuse after her death in 1917. A real estate developer named Arthur Edwards, also an associate of Palmer, acquired the land in the 1930s and advocated for its preservation as a state park, which was successfully accomplished in 1941. (Note that the traditional spelling, *Miakka*, retained in most local signage and used historically by residents, differs from the spelling *Myakka*, appearing on official maps, deeds, and other government and public documents, a discrepancy attributed to a scrivener's error dating to the late 1800s.[75])

The Myakka River originates near the Hardee and Manatee County border and flows seventy-two miles into Charlotte Harbor, alongside the Peace River (traditionally, Peas River). Most of the Myakka River's meanderings are extremely remote. The origin of the unusual Mikosokee name is unknown, though it is thought to derive from the same source as Miami (traditionally Mai-yami).[76]

When exploring the park, if it happens to be May, you can't miss the sea of daffodil-yellow blossoms covering thousands of acres of prairie along Myakka River State Park Road, the park's main artery. May is the month of the Coreopsis, or "tickseed," in Central Florida, a small yellow blossom that for a few short weeks in late spring carpets hundreds of acres of prairie in Miakka. This is an award-winning photography spot (not to mention a popular location for marriage proposals). Another yellow explosion bursts forth at Lake Myakka, where locals enjoy parking and strolling among the yellow blossoms (but watch for rattlers).

South of Lake Myakka, on the east side of the park road, across from Big Flats Marsh, is the gate entrance of Bertha Palmer's historic ranch, Meadowsweet Pastures.[77] No ranch buildings remain here, but a pleasant hike beyond the gate awaits the interested. Also of interest are the cornucopia of artifacts that hikers and visitors have informally assembled, originating at the time of Mrs. Palmer's ranch era. The foundations of some of Mrs. Palmer's former ranch structures are unmarked, unregulated, and free for exploring for anyone willing to hike a mile or so past the gate. Going farther, Ranch House Road connects with a network of primitive trails by way of All-Weather Road. At the park's southern entrance off Clark Road/State Road 72, a large rock marker memorializes the Palmer family's contribution of nearly two thousand acres to the State of Florida.

Myakka River State Park Road crosses the Myakka River just after the pull-off for the Canopy Trail. This is a (in)famous place to view alligators, and there are usually some big granddaddy bull gators, as we used to call them at the University of Florida, that enjoy sunning themselves, especially

A marker commemorates Bertha Palmer's descendants, who donated part of Meadowsweet Acres, her beloved cattle ranch, to the people of Florida for use as a state park. *Author photo.*

Roosevelt's Tree Army (the CCC) contributed several structures to the park that still serve the people of Florida: this primitive cabin, along with four others like it; several park ranger cabins; a barn that is now part of the Myakka Outpost; and the park's main artery—the Myakka River State Park Road. *Author photo.*

on chilly January afternoons. I have personally seen alligators two- and three-thick on the banks of the Myakka River during the winter. It is rare to stop at this bridge and not see at least one alligator snoozing on the bank or stalking waterfowl. However, the legendary spot to view alligators lies outside the park boundaries, off State Road 72 at Lower Myakka Lake, at Deephole, a sinkhole partly submerged by the lake. The sinkhole is 300 feet wide and 130 feet deep, and it is common to see literally hundreds of alligators basking on its shore, especially in the cooler, dryer months. The swampier, hot months make for poor alligator watching: For one, the gators are typically lurking beneath the surface, keeping cool, out of sight. Also, the rainy season (July to October) means the swelling of sloughs and creeks in the gators' habitats, so they are more dispersed and thus less likely to be seen congregated around a single spot like Deephole.[78]

Farther south of the river crossing, Myakka River State Park Road intersects Cabin Road, which consists of a pavilion and a collection of five historic log cabins, still in use as park visitor lodging and always booked solid from November to April. Cabin Road is marked with a small sign just north of the bathrooms and requires a five-minute walk down a dirt road.

Myakka River State Park—not yet quite a tame place—was at least subdued by the Civilian Conservation Corps in the 1930s. Today, its dense undergrowth, thick, dark forests, and prolific population of alligators still leave one agog at the achievements of the young men of the CCC. *Author photo.*

These rustic log cabins were built by the Civilian Conservation Corps (CCC) in the 1930s. The CCC employed young men of approximately eighteen to twenty-five, popularly known as the "CCC boys." Usually from lower-class families, "Roosevelt's tree army" was hired to clear and build infrastructure on public lands throughout the country, including in Myakka, Florida. The CCC paid them a salary of $30 per month, $25 of which they typically sent home to their families in other states, keeping $5 for spending money. In addition to their salary, the boys received room and board, as well as some arithmetic, literacy, and job-skills training. On Saturday nights, the CCC hosted dances for the young men with the young ladies of Sarasota, and it even published a monthly newsletter at one point.[79]

These brave, resilient youngsters cleared the thick, impenetrable, and often dangerous brush, and they built the horse barn that is now part of the Myakka Outpost; the Myakka River State Park Road; the predecessor to the bridge at the river crossing and several others; and the pavilion and log cabins, which are still standing after nearly a century.

Many workers quit due to malaria, dehydration, or heat exhaustion, and several photos remain of a group holding ten-foot water moccasins as big around as tree trunks, slain in the course of the CCC's labors for the park. The sturdy, honest design of the structures still in use today and the drive along the winding, often dark and mysterious park road attest to the industry and grit of a former generation.

CENTRAL LAKES REGION

30

MARJORIE KINNAN RAWLINGS'S *THE YEARLING* TRAIL

Cross Creek is both a waterway and a community: The small stream connects Lochloosa Lake and Orange Lake, and the tiny settlement grew up as a fishing camp on its banks. Cross Creek was made famous in the stories and characters of Marjorie Kinnan Rawlings, who lived here from 1929 to 1948. Rawlings even named one of her books, *Cross Creek*, after this community. Her most famous novel, *The Yearling*, won a Pulitzer Prize in 1939.

A native of Washington, D.C., and a graduate of the University of Wisconsin, Rawlings, at the age of thirty-two, along with her first husband, Charles, purchased a thirty-acre orange grove on Orange Lake. At that time, orange groves stretched the width of the isthmus, from Orange Lake to Lochloosa Lake, and the Rawlingses expected to live off income from the groves and to retreat to the quiet farm to write.

Rawlings discovered the real gem lay not in the citrus fruit but in the people of Cross Creek, who became the chief subject of her numerous books. Part sociologist, part naturalist, part fiction writer, Rawlings testifies to the many and varied lives and experiences of the Florida Crackers who comprised the citizenry of the state prior to the advent of Walt Disney, Carnival Cruise, and Miami Beach. Rawlings lived here for most of the remainder of her life. She died in 1953 but left her entire property to the University of Florida, which honored her in the naming of Rawlings Hall.

Her farmhouse, kitchen garden, flower gardens, orange groves, tenant house, barn, and outbuildings are administered by the state park and are open to the public. The beautifully furnished interior of the farmhouse, containing exclusively Rawlings's original belongings, is accessible only as part of a docent-led tour.

Of special interest is the farm kitchen and its tiny woodstove, with which Rawlings developed the recipes for her excellent, painstakingly researched cookbook, *Cross Creek Cookery*. A beautiful edition is available from Fireside Publishers and is worth every cent of the cover price. The mingling of rich local history, food, and literature in the book is an exhaustive look at authentic Florida cooking, well beyond the Cross Creek area. As a native of Tampa, I especially enjoyed her introduction to "Mrs. Chancey's Spanish Bean Soup" on page 7:

> *As happy a gustatory experience as can come to mortal man, is to sit down in one of the Cuban restaurants in Tampa and eat all one can hold of Spanish bean soup.... With the soup goes the hot Cuban bread, thick and crisp of crust, delicate of interior, served hot enough to burn the fingers in the six-inch portions wrapped in a paper towel. The waiter, who looks like King Alfonso, will fill your bowl from a great silver tureen as often as it is empty.... Cubans and* [Tampanians] *are generous folk, and I have been able to bring home to the Creek backwoods the recipes for these hearty and delicious soups. Those of the mayor's wife are the best in Tampa.*[80]

I also enjoy her menu suggestions; here's one from her book:

> *Greek Lemon Soup (see page 10)*
> *Blackbird Pie (the vegetables are in it) (see page 119)*
> *Mixed Green or Combination Salad*
> *Sweet Potato Pone (see page 183)*[81]

Back in Rawlings's kitchen, it was at this very table that the Rawlingses hosted notable writers and artists including Zora Neale Hurston. The table is laid with one of the three sets of Rawlings's own fine china, which she used daily, and her original linens and flatware; much of her actual cookware and utensils hangs on the walls. Of course, and most notably, she wrote her beloved coming-of-age novel *The Yearling* here in this 1884 board-and-batten farmhouse.

The Yearling portrays a single year in the life of a fictional family, the Baxters, who are based on the 1880s family of Ruben and Sara Long. The Long family homestead is forty miles southeast of here between Fort McCoy and Lake George. The buildings are no longer extant, but their family cemetery and a few primitive trails with landmarks from the novel are maintained by the Ocala National Forest on the Yearling Trail. Rawlings lived with the Longs for several months as she researched setting and mood, developed her characters, and immersed herself in the people and the ecology of what would become the backdrop for *The Yearling*.

If it's not summertime and you brought your walking shoes, it might be worth your while to take the hour detour and visit the Yearling Trail—trailhead located off FL-19. The trail is a five-mile loop through the Florida scrub; parts of it offer no shade, so bring plenty of water and insect repellent. The only historical site is the Long family cemetery, but the hike offers a real look at the factual setting of *The Yearling*.[82]

Silver Glen Run is located across US-19 from the trailhead. Rawlings opens *The Yearling* with the young protagonist, Jody, fleeing his afternoon chores down the path to the nearby spring, where he falls asleep in a cradle of palmetto brush. He awakens hours later, after dusk, to find the footsteps of a doe scattered about him, foreshadowing his later meeting with that very doe's fawn. The cool and quiet waterway where he falls asleep in the brush and first encounters the doe is Silver Glen Run.

The white-tailed deer or *Odocoileus virginianus* is ubiquitous in rural Florida. The variety commonly seen grazing silently among the Florida brush is smaller and lighter than its northern counterpart, and its antlers are smaller and less impressive, with only two or three points at most.

Later in the novel, Jody befriends the orphan fawn, which he raises and keeps as a pet for one year. At the end of the year, Jody must sacrifice the deer, now a yearling, to save the cornfield that is his family's only livelihood. In putting down the pet he cherishes so much to ensure his family's survival, young Jody emerges from boyhood, becoming a man. A poignant coming-of-age novel, *The Yearling* was made into a movie starring Gregory Peck in 1946.

Rawlings is said to have insisted that Sidney Franklin and Clarence Brown film on-site, among her beloved north-central Florida sand pine scrub. Today Rawlings is credited with documenting the history, flora, and fauna of this part of Florida. She was also a force in its preservation, since prior to her writing, life in this remote area of the Florida scrub was consigned to the most downtrodden—those who could afford to live nowhere else.

North of Marjorie Kinnan Rawlings State Park, County Road 325 curves left, leading to The Yearling Restaurant and Cabins. The Yearling Restaurant opened in 1952, six years after the filming of the movie. The restaurant is located on the banks of Cross Creek, and the splendor of the majestic ancient oaks draped with Spanish moss against the silent, dark water of the age-old connector waterway takes your breath away. The restaurant hours mimic those of the state park: it opens for lunch at noon, Thursdays through Sundays only (but it does not close, as the historic home tour does, for August and September).

The restaurant offers a unique experience, combining the literary, the historical, and the culinary. Prior to the opening of the restaurant, this spot on the creek was home to an old fish camp, and a few buildings are extant from this prior era. Now, The Yearling offers truly Southern cuisine (pork ribeye, fried alligator, fried catfish, and roasted venison are its most popular entrées) in an authentically old-Florida environment.

Cozy dining areas unfold one after another, most walls lined from floor to ceiling with used books, many of them rare first editions or signed by the author (a small sign advises every book on premises is for sale—The Yearling is also a used bookstore). Abounding in niches and covering the walls is memorabilia from the 1947 film; Rawlings's estate; and, of course, Jody Baxter and the novel.

To the left of the hostess stand is a cozy, old-fashioned bar. Beyond this, the creaky wooden floors in a narrow hallway lined with vintage, hardcover books lead to the back dining area, also a music hall, the centerpiece of which is a ten-foot stuffed alligator. A blues band offers live music here each evening. Stuffed bobcats, Florida wild boar, deer, and other game are displayed throughout the restaurant, evoking the feel of a vintage hunting lodge.

No less charming than the cafe are the rentable miniature cabins nearby, with quaint, literary-minded names like *South Moon Under*, a royal blue bungalow named after Rawlings's novella about moonshiners, and *When the Whippoorwills*, a yellow block tiny house, evoking her collection of short stories by that name. Each cabin has a private bath and a kitchenette. The friendly hostess, a fisherwoman herself, noted that everyone from anglers, hunters, and sportfishermen, to University of Florida students and professors and vacationing families just passing through, are common lodgers here.

31
THE TOWN THAT TIME FORGOT

When William Bartram arrived at the outskirts of what is now the tiny town known as Micanopy, a mile from the capital city of the Alachua Tribe, he was cheerfully greeted by a few Indian women and children who inhabited three or four dwellings. Nearby was "a noble forest of orange grove." He also observed that "near the path was a large artificial mound of earth…supposed to be the work of ancient Floridians or Yamasees, with other traces of an Indian town."[83]

The Indian mound Bartram discovered is just a few feet from the parking area off SE Tuscawilla Road, northwest of the informational kiosk, a raised area behind the fence and the sign. A quiet nature trail leads back into the pine woods, but it isn't marked and is overgrown in certain parts. Not much to see, but those so inclined can enjoy the terrain, flora, and fauna that the Alachua people likely experienced as residents of Tuscawilla in the late 1700s.

The Native women told Bartram of the capital of the Alachua Seminole Tribe. He goes on, "After riding near a mile farther, we arrived at Cuscowilla.…Near the banks, a pretty brook of water ran through the town, and entered the lake just by."[84]

Bartram had arrived at just about where the town of Micanopy (MIK-uh-noh-pee) sits today, where he was greeted by Chief Cowkeeper. Cowkeeper was amused upon hearing of Bartram's mission but approved and dubbed him Puc Puggy, or "Flower-Hunter," a name memorialized by a road and boat ramp in Paynes Prairie. Cowkeeper showed Bartram gracious hospitality, offering him and his party the peace pipe and a generous bowl of "thin drink." Bartram goes on to recount an idyllic life led by a prosperous, isolated tribe in a village of thirty dwellings, each one about thirty by twelve feet typically with two sections. The first of these was a kitchen and lodging area and the second a common room for the head of the household to receive guests and relax.[85]

Bartram's journals describing events like his reception by Cowkeeper, published in 1791 and freely available in the public domain, are the primary accounts of Seminole tribal culture in Micanopy in the late 1700s.

The town's namesake is the Seminole Chief Micanopy, a descendant of Old Chief Cowkeeper and of King Payne. Chief Micanopy was the nominal head of the Seminole Nation in the 1820s, when the United States took possession of Florida from the Spanish.[86] He was described as a self-indulgent, heavy man who espoused pacifist views only because of his own unfitness for combat. However, he was lenient with his inferiors due to his phlegmatic disposition, and one Indian agent described him as communicative and good-tempered. Another contemporary said of him that when "Micanopy spoke, all must obey." He kept many slaves and large herds of cattle and ponies.

The Indian Removal Act was in full force at this time in Florida, and the United States had been working to expel the last three hundred Seminole tribal members from the new territory, which resulted in the Second Seminole War. Finally, in 1837, under a flag truce, Chief Micanopy attended a talk with U.S. officials. Despite the truce, U.S. troops ambushed him and took him to St. Augustine, to be shipped to Fort Moultrie and then to Oklahoma. (His portrait was taken by George Catlin, noted painter of Native Americans, at Fort Moultrie in South Carolina just before he was shipped west to Oklahoma.) He is said to have wept at his departure. Chief Micanopy died in Oklahoma ten years later.

Today, Micanopy is a one-square-mile incorporated town of about 700, and it is the oldest inland settlement in Florida. It lies between Ocala and Gainesville, just south of Paynes Prairie, an ancient sinkhole known by historic tribes as the "Great Alachua Savannah." There is no school, no hospital or doctors' offices, no stoplights, no jails. Therefore, Micanopy is popularly known as "the town that time forgot." Much like Cedar Key, Micanopy is a destination for University of Florida professors and students who want to escape the hustle and bustle of the 100,000-person college town a few miles north. It's probably best known for the Historic Micanopy Cemetery with markers dating to the early 1800s.

Bartram's Trail to Chief Cowkeeper's chiefdom in the heart of Micanopy took him west on present-day SE Tuscawilla Road about half a mile to the intersection at Connell Circle. Just before the intersection sits a stone well known as the Territorial Well. It was used by the Spanish and is the only structure still standing that predated the platting of Micanopy in 1880. No sign marks the well, and it's easy to miss, unless you know where to look. "Territorial" designates a structure that originated in Florida's period as a U.S. territory, before statehood in 1845.[87]

WANTON'S PLACE

Beyond the Territorial Well is the oldest house in Micanopy, the Stewart-Merry House (1855), now a private residence. John Merry's children were the neighborhood kids who found colorful beads and pottery shards on the Indian mound back at Tuscawilla Preserve. The location of the Stewart-Merry House at the corner of Cholokka Boulevard and East Ocala Avenue is the probable location of the original trading post here, the first successful European settlement in Micanopy. It has since been completely destroyed, but its presence was key to the settling of the town of Micanopy. Known on early maps as merely "Wanton's" or "Wanton's Place," its location approximately halfway between St. Augustine and Tallahassee, in the precise center of La Florida, made it a key hub for traders, early pioneers, soldiers, cowhunters, and Seminoles.

Edward Mills Wanton was a British Loyalist who arrived in the Micanopy area in the 1820s, drawn like Chief Cowkeeper by the rich grazing lands of the Great Savannah. Wanton was the sole white settler in the Micanopy area: most of his household were free or enslaved Blacks, and all his neighbors were Seminoles and free or enslaved people of color, the latter of whom had joined Seminole tribes as a quasi-servant class.

Wanton later acted as a mediator between local tribal leaders and white outsiders who wished to develop North Central Florida, particularly Moses Elias Levy. His friendly and often conciliatory relationship with powerful Seminole chiefs later incurred the wrath of Governor Andrew Jackson, who labeled Wanton a profligate and ordered him jailed.

Wanton's Place also hosted community meetings, nascent town council meetings, and Sunday services when the occasional circuit preacher made his way down to the area. An 1826 correspondence referenced a post office at "Wanton's" as well. He left numerous ancestors in this area, many of whom were of mixed-race.

Wanton passed away quietly in 1839, and his entire compound was burned by U.S. soldiers during the Second Seminole War to prevent the Indians from using it as a fortification. Nothing is left of his compound, but he is considered the founder of Micanopy by some.

This intersection of Cholokka Boulevard and East Ocala Avenue was also the probable location of Fort Defiance and later Fort Micanopy, both of which played a role in the Seminole Wars of the 1800s. These too were strategically burned in the Second Seminole War by U.S. troops.

Making a right on Cholokka Boulevard, you are now entering the mile-square Micanopy Historic District on the National Register of Historic Places.[88] First is the "prettiest home in Alachua County," the Simonton House, an elaborate Queen Anne–style mansion located at 101 Northeast Cholokka Boulevard. Heading north, on your right are the two main restaurants here, Coffee n' Cream in the Shady Oak Gallery, and Old Florida Cafe next door, both delightful lunch options. The front porch of Coffee n' Cream often hosts local bluegrass bands during the lunch hour, even on weekdays. The Shady Oak Gallery was built in the 1980s but is an exact replica of the historic Gibson Inn, circa 1907, located in Apalachicola, near Tallahassee.

Across the median on the left is the "downtown business district" of Micanopy, a row of flat brick buildings in some places completely overtaken by vines. These include the Micanopy Banking Company Building (1906), the Benjamin Building (1885), and the Feaster Building (1902). The Dailey Drug Store, farther down Cholokka Boulevard, caps the "business block," picturesquely framed with ancient oak trees heavily laden with Spanish moss—the second-most-photographed spot in Micanopy. (The first is undoubtedly the Historic Micanopy Cemetery, a separate listing on the National Register.)

STEAMBOAT *CHACALA*

A park-like median divides Cholokka Boulevard, the town's informal "Main Street," displaying the steamboat *Chacala* anchor among the azaleas and park benches. Sometime around the 1870s, locals noticed the Great Savannah, now known as Paynes Prairie, seemed rainier than usual.[89] The typical winter pattern of receding ponds and marshes giving way to dry prairie was broken. Cattlemen groused about the standing water there all year-round; they soon weren't able to graze their stock there.

By the 1880s, Paynes Prairie was known as Alachua Lake. The lake was so vast that at one point sailboats traversed both where US-441 and Interstate 75 now cross the prairie. This was in some ways a good thing; a boat is much more convenient for transporting freight than a mule wagon drawn over sand. However, the new lake also caused problems; cattlemen now had to graze their stock on higher, less nutritious pinewood flats and scrub brush. (Rural, thinly populated Florida didn't repeal its statewide No-Fence laws until 1949.)

In response to the flooding of Paynes Prairie, one Captain James Coxton operated the steamboat *Chacala*, which he built himself for hauling both oranges and passengers across the lake. The Alachua Sink opened in the early 1890s, and the *Chacala* was marooned southeast of Gainesville, on the other side of Paynes Prairie. This anchor was recovered, but the small shipwreck still rests somewhere at the bottom of Biven's Arm in Gainesville, among the alligators and white ibises.

North on Cholokka Boulevard is the Herlong Mansion, a Colonial-style brick mansion constructed in 1915. The Greek Revival brick façade encases the original 1875 wood-frame vernacular structure, but the heart pine floors upstairs are original. The Herlong Mansion is now a bed-and-breakfast, with private baths in each room. The current owners have painstakingly preserved the home's historical integrity while making it accessible to modern clientele. For example, on the first floor is a handicap-accessible shower, large enough for a guest with a wheelchair, yet the ambience is still distinctly turn of the century.

A HISTORIC WALKING TOUR

Farther down Cholokka Boulevard (sometimes called just Main Street by locals) is the Thrasher Warehouse, now the Micanopy Historical Society Museum, where an excellent historic sites map is available. The National Register listing for the Micanopy Historic District observes two unifying elements of the original plan of Micanopy. First, one can look down each major boulevard and see a notable residence. For example, looking south down Cholokka Boulevard, the Stewart-Merry House is in view. At the end of Ocala Avenue is the JW Barr House. Second, the town custom at the time of its platting was for the business owner to reside across the street from his place of business. Directly across from the Thrasher Store (1912) is the Thrasher family home (1900) at the corner of Northeast Fifth and Cholokka Boulevard. Captain Fontaine's Queen Anne–style home, now an antique store, was across the street from the park-like greenspace, once home to the Fontaine General Store, near 304 Cholokka Boulevard. One may view the brick foundations of the latter amid the grassy vacant lot. Changes over the last century since its 1880 platting have somewhat altered these unifying elements, but a keen eye on the walking tour will see evidence of the original intent of the city planners.

Next to the museum is the Roberts House, circa 1910, now home to a bakehouse; across the street is the Old Brick Schoolhouse, now city hall. Today, Micanopy children attend school in Gainesville, ten miles north of here. To follow the walking tour from city hall, retrace your steps less than a block to the intersection of Bay and Cholokka, and head down Northeast Seventh Avenue. After one block, make a left at Division Street and head south about six city blocks to where it ends on Smith Avenue; here turn left. At 107 Smith Avenue is the former Micanopy Baptist Church, built in the 1880s. It is now a private residence.

Heading east on Smith Avenue, follow it as it turns left and then make a right at Ocala Avenue. The Barr House's (1911) Victorian predecessor was lost to a fire, the fate of several beautiful old homes here in Micanopy. John Jacob Barr and his family arrived in Micanopy in the 1850s, moving from South Carolina. You may notice the home looks relatively modern: Members of the Barr family didn't want their home to succumb to a fire again and used more modern building materials in the construction of their second home on this site.

But it's not the architecture we are most interested in here: the centuries-old oak trees standing in the front yard of the home are said to be Chief Micanopy's Council Oaks. Here the old Indian chief cut deals with white men, formulated tribal agendas with his subchiefs, and hosted and entertained counterpart chiefs of other regional tribes. Pause here a moment and imagine the saga to which these giant oaks were witnesses: old Chief Cowkeeper's reign; Wanton's bustling Indian outpost; the garrison marching drills under the auspices of Fort Defiance, later to be utterly destroyed by U.S. troops before they evacuated to Fort Marion; Chief Micanopy's downfall and poignant final surrender; his tragic expulsion from his tribal homelands; then the entrance of the Americans of European extraction, including the

Barr family, who in 1891 lost their precious daughter Gertrude Annie Barr in the house that preceded the current structure.

"Miss Annie" was just seventeen when she succumbed to pneumonia. The Barrs then lost their family home to a catastrophic fire in the early 1900s. A photograph from about 1880 shows Miss Annie as a small child with one of her siblings. The two children peek out from among the immense branches of one of the oak trees, the original old Victorian Barr home visible in the background.

Retrace your steps back to Smith Avenue, this time crossing the intersection with Division Street to the still-handsome ruins of an old brick wall where Northwest Second Street intersects with Smith Avenue. Here at 201 West Smith Avenue was the homesite of Dr. and Mrs. Lucius Montgomery, but fire destroyed three successive Victorian houses here, all owned by the Montgomery family.

A contemporary account describes the first one as "two stories high with a two-story cupola, having every convenience and comfort, surrounded by orange groves."[90] It was destroyed by a fire in 1895 but was rebuilt soon after. The second home went up in flames in 1911. "Both of these houses were set far back behind the brick fence and a long walk under spreading chinquapin trees led up to the entrance, which was always framed with magnificent blue hydrangeas in the spring and early summer."[91] A third house was constructed, but a final fire claimed this last house in the 1930s.

Three catastrophic fires destroying the family home are too much for any family; a fourth dwelling was never constructed, and the lot has remained vacant for nearly one hundred years now. The classic brick gate, with a capstone dated 1897, remained standing until the late 1990s, when a road improvement project caused a massive oak tree to fall and damage parts of it. A trust was established to preserve the landmark, an effort now known as the Montgomery Wall Project. Today, the Montgomery Wall is a protected historic landmark with funding in place to preserve this iconic reminder of a bygone era for generations to come.

MICANOPY HISTORIC CEMETERY

The final stop on the walking tour of Micanopy is Gertrude Annie Barr's gravestone, enclosed in the hauntingly beautiful Micanopy Historic Cemetery, right next door to the Montgomery Wall. Dr. and Mrs. Lucius

Montgomery gifted the land for the cemetery to the Town of Micanopy in 1897.

Stepping inside the gate of this cemetery makes the Micanopy historic walking tour come alive (for lack of a better expression!). Misty and green all twelve months of the year, quiet and lonely at every hour of the day, sacred and shadowy, eerie and still—it is hard to believe that a mere ten miles from this spot, some of the faithful departed's descendants are ninety-six thousand strong at a deafening college football game in Gainesville.

If you spend enough time here and have the interest, you could literally trace every dwelling and structure on your historical society museum map to a family plot or at least a single gravestone in this cemetery. Look for the Merry, Stewart, Simonton, Thrasher, Barr, Fontaine, and Herlong family plots, many enclosed in somber wrought-iron gates.

The earliest gravestone in this cemetery was erected in 1826, an extremely early date for a Florida cemetery; Florida wasn't admitted as a state until 1845 and had only become a U.S. territory in 1821. This earliest soul was James William Martin (1737–1826); little is known about who he was or how he came to live (and die) at such a remote part of Central Florida at his advanced age. (Recall that the first European settler, Edward Wanton of the original trading outpost "Wantons," was just establishing his settlement here in the early 1820s.)

Of special interest is the lovely enclosed garden of the Barr family plot. Young Annie Barr's gravestone is the most photographed site in Micanopy; some of the antique shops even incorporate a sketch or profile of the stone angel in their windows and signs. To find it, head to the southeastern quadrant of the cemetery and look for the stone angel holding a flower-festooned cross. The figure points menacingly upward as it looks down at passersby, as if to say, "Little Miss Annie died young and good; are you, her survivor, making good use of the time you have left?"

32

DORA DRAWDY'S "MOUNTAIN" HOMESTEAD

It was the early 1840s, and James Drawdy and his twenty-year-old wife, Dora Ann, heard of an opportunity to stake a claim in the territory *of La Florida*, which the United States had just obtained from the Spanish.[92] It wasn't yet settled except for some plantations along the border and a few military outposts. They moved their family from southern Georgia, past the crooked, dark Suwannee River; they also passed a gentle plateau overlooking a magnificent lake, sheltered by friendly pine trees and ancient oaks. They staked their claim just beyond the lake, at a narrow piece of land separating it from the smaller Lake Beauclair. They built a cabin of pine logs, installed fencing to corral their livestock, and eventually planted grapefruit trees and operated a cotton gin.

In 1848, the federal government sent a surveying crew headed up by deputy surveyor C.C. Tracy to the newly minted La Florida. He found little evidence of human activity for a few long weeks as he forged a trail through the northern Florida wilderness, mainly pine forest. According to Tracy's field notes, the crew finally came to a wagon road and then a hammock (a small hill covered with trees), finally ending at the shore of a large lake. On the other side of this lake was a charming cabin, a homesteader from Georgia, his sweet farm wife, their eight children, and a hot meal. Dora Ann Drawdy was said to have laundered (what by that time must have been filthy) clothes and cooked meals for him and his crew. The Drawdys allowed the surveying crewmen to camp on their land for the duration of their fieldwork, and for this act of disinterested Christian courtesy, the surveyor named the largest of the two lakes Lake Dora.

Dora's husband left to join the Confederate forces and was later killed at Fredericksburg in December 1862. Now a widow, Dora moved her family to a more settled area known at that time as Seneca, about six miles north of modern-day Mount Dora. She is buried at the lonely Umatilla Cemetery north of Mount Dora in Umatilla. Like many Florida small towns, Umatilla has five large cemeteries, despite its current population of less than four thousand. This incongruity bears witness to its high point in the citrus boom, which declined in the last half of the twentieth century.

In its infancy, Mount Dora was visited annually by the traveling Chautauqua folk festivals, which circulated among rural areas of the United States with the purpose of educating, inspiring, and instructing pioneer communities. In *A Brief History of Mount Dora, Florida*, the authors aptly describe the Chautauqua traveling camps as a "pioneer version of a TED talk and a big tent revival, mixed together with Wikipedia and Woodstock."[93] These gatherings became immensely popular in Mount Dora at the turn of the century.

Today, Mount Dora is a very special place. The major north–south Highway 441 that cuts through most of the state bypasses Mount Dora, which allowed the town to grow organically without much interference from the outside after the decline of the railway system in the 1940s. The Chautauqua meetings of its early years gave rise to a warm sense of place, community education, and a distinct appreciation—and even affection—for local culture. Its identity as the "Festival Town" is one outcome of this spunky sense of place, with nearly every weekend of the year boasting some minor or major arts and crafts festival, regatta, tour of homes, or holiday parade.

A note on geography: the town overlooks Lake Dora as a preacher might cast his gaze over his congregation from the pulpit. At 188 feet above sea level, Mount Dora is not a mountain, yet Florida boasts few higher spots. The elevation rises gently over the hills of FL-46 as you drive along the pretty country roads. Only when you stand at the Mount Dora Town Hall and look down on Lake Dora does the "mountain" title make sense. (The highest point in Florida is Britton Hill, in Walton County near the Georgia border, 345 feet above sea level.)

Lakeside Inn (1883), formerly the Alexander House, overlooks the majestic Lake Dora opening expansively beyond. The Alexander House was a private residence, built mainly to entertain the owner's friends and family from up north. Soon he began renting rooms and offering meals, and the boardinghouse gradually assumed the ambience of a resort, as more visitors came to Mount Dora for pleasure. Its early guests from the North would have arrived by steamship, having disembarked a train or steamer in Jacksonville and boarded a smaller steamboat at the St. John's River to continue the 140-mile waterborne journey to Mount Dora. The steamboat carried them southwest "up" the river (the St. John's River is one of only a handful of rivers in the United States that flows north) to the Harris Chain of Lakes, which includes Lake Dora. Here, weary natives of Ohio, New York, and New England would have finally disembarked at Lakeside Inn, having endured over a week of travel to reach their destination. Today, Lakeside Inn enjoys the prestigious distinction of being Florida's oldest continuously running hotel. President Calvin Coolidge stayed here for a month with the first family in January 1929.

North of the inn is the hexagonal Historic Train Depot. In 1915, the Atlantic Coast Line Railroad replaced the existing rectangular building with a unique segmented arch wall system. The immense success of the Chautauqua festivals and the booming citrus packing operation meant numerous visitors arrived daily in the scenic lake town by rail. This increase in traffic demanded an update to the train depot; the town of Mount Dora had proven that it was here to stay. The train depot today houses the Mount Dora Chamber of Commerce. The railway bridge over Tremain south of the depot evokes images of an 1880s steam locomotive powering through the bamboo and the palm trees, carrying passengers southwest from Jacksonville.

A quarter of a mile farther on Tremain is the Grantham Pointe Lighthouse. Built in 1988, the lighthouse isn't exactly a historical monument, but the five acres of Gilbert Park from which its small jetty protrudes were donated by the son of Dr. Calvin Gilbert, one of Mount Dora's earliest residents. The thirty-five-foot lighthouse is registered as an inland aid to boaters navigating Lake Dora after dusk. Gilbert Park and the "Mt. Dora Lighthouse" are reportedly the best place in town to take in a sunset, though a west-facing rocking chair from Lakeside Inn's expansive verandah a few blocks north of here is a close second.

The most unique structure in Mount Dora proper today is the Donnelly House, built in 1879 by one J.P. Donnelly. This magnificent residence is an example of Steamboat Gothic architecture, which emerged in the 1850s when the steam-powered scroll saw enabled the large-scale production of ornately carved banisters and balustrades. Donnelly, like many of his contemporaries, was a great admirer of steamboats, usually ornamented with elaborate lacy wood detailing and other flamboyant

Above: The thirty-five-foot Lake Dora Lighthouse (1988), though not quite a historic structure, is registered as an inland aid for mariners boating among the Harris Chain of Lakes after dusk. *Author photo.*

Left: Central Florida architecture doesn't often draw on the Steamboat Gothic, but the Donnelly House in Mount Dora is a delightful exception. Also known as Carpenter Gothic, this design evolved from the abundance of timber in North America and the invention of the steam-powered scroll saw, resulting in the mass production of the elaborate detailing elements of its typical façade. *Author photo.*

flourishes. He and many others paid homage to this innovative yet stylish means of transportation by incorporating colorful steamboat detailing into their residences.

A hexagonal turret dominates its aspect when approaching from the south, balanced by numerous gables of varying size, with white lacy wooden detailing and numerous small scalloped shingles, curlicue flourishes, and ornate spindles adorning its multiple balconies. While Steamboat Gothic architecture is principally found in structures in the Mississippi and Ohio River Valleys, it's easy to understand why gentlemen like J.P. Donnelly, and his real estate–minded wife, Annie Stone MacDonald, wanted to pay homage to the steamboat in a home built on the shores of the Harris Chain of Lakes, accessible chiefly by steam in the late 1800s.

The Donnelly House sits among colorful storefronts and historic dwellings in Mount Dora's historic district. Dora Drawdy Way connects Alexander Street and North Donnelly Street at West Third Avenue. The name of this tiny byway marks a gesture of appreciation to Mount Dora's namesake. Day-trippers have their pick of colorful eateries, distilleries, and coffeehouses located in vintage houses, from Maw's Mountain Moonshine located in the 1922 Child's House to PizzAmore on East Fifth Avenue a few blocks east of downtown. Too many vintage establishments to name occupy these historical spaces and nooks, quiet brick roads, and colorful courtyards of adorable, historical Mount Dora.

33

LONGWOOD

"THE SENATOR" TURNS 3,500

A tragic death occurred near this spot in Longwood in 2012, but the victim was neither man nor beast. The scene of the crime: Big Tree Park north of Longwood, Florida. "The Senator," an estimated 3,500-year-old bald cypress tree, had been a landmark for Seminole Indian tribes for centuries before white men saw it for the first time. Pioneer mapping and early surveys referenced the magnificent natural landmark, an informal tourist destination even back when visitors had to jump from log to log across swampland for access.

Although a hurricane in 1925 destroyed the top branches, lopping off about 50 feet and reducing its height to 118 feet, the ancient cypress was still a prized arbor. Senator Moses Overstreet donated it and the surrounding land for use as a park in 1927. In 1929, President Calvin Coolidge visited the park and the old tree, which had by that time been nicknamed "The Senator" after its prior owner.

The Senator thrived here in the middle of this lonely peninsula, even settling down with a nearby 2,000-year-old bald cypress named "Lady Liberty," about 40 feet from the old Senator. In 2012, an unattended campfire finally took down the old man at the ripe old age of 3.5 millennia, leaving Lady Liberty a bereaved widow.

Shortly after the incident, Seminole County planted near the Big Tree Park parking area a sapling of the same species, dubbing it "The Phoenix." It's to be found there today, behind a black wrought-iron fence similar to the barrier that encircled the Senator. But the defining feature of this area is gone, and this rugged and wild landscape is forever altered.

SEABOARD AIRLINE RAILROAD CORRIDOR

Sanford, Longwood, Maitland, Winter Park, and Kissimmee form a railroad corridor down the high spine of Central Florida, each owing its genesis to the Seaboard Airline Railroad, the original railroad connecting Northerners to America's "Winter Playground" in the late nineteenth and early twentieth centuries. The *airline* part of the name comes from its being advertised as an arrow-straight railroad connecting New York and Florida by the shortest possible route, "straight as a plumb line."

Train was replacing the steamboat as the snowbird vehicle of choice when Peter Demens of St. Petersburg, Russia, came to America. He arrived in 1881 in New York City and immediately headed for a relative's orange plantation in Jacksonville. Jacksonville prices proved too high for the Russian expat, so he boarded a steamboat headed for the remote center of the state and ended up in Longwood, where land was cheaper. He opened a sawmill that supplied the Orange Belt Railway with railway ties and also furnished building material for Rollins College, located south of Longwood in Winter Park. Demens's narrow-gauge railway eventually connected Sanford and St. Petersburg in Pinellas County. A narrow-gauge railway is lighter and cheaper than a standard railway and is ideal for uneven or mountainous terrain. However, the railcars hold fewer passengers, and most significantly, the reduced stability of the lightweight cars means lower speeds.[94]

"Lady Liberty," a 2,000-year-old bald cypress at Big Tree Park in Longwood, survived "The Senator," 3,500 years old, which burned in a campfire in 2012. The Senator and Lady Liberty are recorded among the oldest known Seminole histories of the landscape of this area, having served as landmarks by the earliest human occupants of Central Florida. *Author photo.*

As Demens was at work on the Orange Belt, Boston native Ed Henck, president of the company that owned the Seaboard Air Line, sought to attract Northerners to the remote

Florida frontier.[95] In 1886, he commissioned the building of a three-story Italianate hotel, which he named the Waltham, after a historic district in Boston. He advertised the Waltham as the sister establishment of a similarly situated hotel in New Hampshire run by the same proprietor. This "pairing" of hotels in the North with a counterpart in the Sunshine State became common in hotel management after the beginning of the twentieth century.

A hotel sitting in the middle of a bald cypress swamp wasn't enough of an attractive vacation destination, so Henck planned the town of Longwood around the hotel and the small wooden train depot. Like Waltham, he named Longwood after yet another charming historic district outside of his native Boston, again echoing the practice of matching towns from New England with a Southern winter counterpart.

After the Great Freeze of 1894 and 1895, which crippled the citrus industry in Orange County, the Waltham closed. Later in the 1920s, it reopened as the St. George Inn and then in 1926 was acquired by a hotel syndicate that included baseball great Joe Tinker as an owner. The group renamed the hotel what would become its permanent designation, the Longwood Hotel. During this time, it enjoyed a brief stint as the Orange and Black, during which time the property became a hub for Prohibition-era antics, described by one account: "Bootleg whiskey, gambling and painted ladies were all popular and available at the Inn."[96]

Located off North Ronald Reagan Boulevard (formerly Old Dixie Highway), Longwood Hotel was sold for use as an office park in 1983. Due to its 1984 enrollment on the National Register, its modern usage exists alongside its historic trappings. The site of the original Longwood train depot (extant but since relocated) is near the Church Avenue railroad crossing.

The Bradlee-McIntyre House

In 1880, Anna M. Bradlee, wife of a prominent Boston architect, purchased a plot of land from a developer in Altamonte Springs, what had become another small winter vacation town, four miles south of Longwood. On her plot, Bradlee commissioned the design and construction of a "gingerbread" Victorian home, characteristic of the ornate homes of the American Gilded Age following the War Between the States.

Known to stay occasionally at the Altamonte Springs Hotel, Civil War General (and future president) Ulysses S. Grant reportedly dropped in to visit the Bradlees and their guests at Anna Bradlee's winter residence across the street. Grant's wife and son are said to have been frequent guests of the Bradlee family in the 1890s.

The McIntyre family purchased the home in 1940, and they were excellent stewards of the structure and grounds until a fatal illness compelled them to sell it in 1967. In 1970, the Victorian mansion was relocated to Longwood's designated historic district, next to the Longwood Hotel, where historic preservation codes would protect it from razing for new development, the fate it faced in Altamonte Springs. According to its entry in the National Register of Historic Places, the Bradlee-McIntyre House is the only remaining example of the flamboyant, ornate Gilded Age–style winter residential structures that dominated the Central Florida landscape toward the end of the nineteenth century.

The elaborate architecture of the Bradlee-McIntyre House inspired the design of the well-executed Longwood Community Building (2002), which sits one block to its west. To the north a few steps away is Christ Church (1881). The architectural style is pioneer chapel, and the interior of the church has many original furnishings, including an altar and lectern even older than the building, gifted to the new congregation by an existing Sanford congregation at its founding. Christ Church was named after Ed Henck's Episcopal church in Longwood, Massachusetts.

MAITLAND

Before Central Florida towns were a series of whistlestops on the Seaboard Airline Railway, they were connected military outposts, small wooden forts constructed in the utter wilderness, usually in response to conflicts of the Seminole War. Lake Lily Drive of Maitland (1885), a small town a few miles south of Longwood, lies on a former military route used in the Second Seminole War connecting Fort Melon (now Sanford) and Fort Gatlin (now Orlando). Later, early pioneers recognized Fort Maitland as the halfway point between the nascent towns, so a farmer transporting crops for sale in Sanford, the closest trade hub, aimed to reach Fort Maitland by noon. No residences existed between Sanford and Orlando until the 1880s, so the sight of Lake Lily and Fort Maitland was a welcome one to lone travelers. The site of the 1838 fort (not extant) is across Orlando Avenue at Fort Maitland Park on Lake Maitland.

For decades, Lake Lily was known as John's Watering Hole. The early settler was homesteading on Lake Conway close to Fort Gatlin (Orlando). One hot morning, he left his wife and children with an oxcart of chickens to peddle at the poultry market in Sanford. Reaching the halfway point of Fort Maitland, John's team spied Lake Lily and charged the watering hole, desperate to drink and cool off. The oxen and chickens perished; John escaped drowning but just barely. He made it back to Orlando on foot, and for decades after, Lake Lily was known as John's Hole in remembrance of his misfortune.[97]

In 1916, Lake Lily Drive became the first brick and grout road in the state of Florida, and in 1927, it was joined to the historic Black Bear Trail. This highway through the habitat of the black bear (*Ursus americanus*) at one time connected Quebec, Canada, to St. Petersburg, Florida, along scenic, heavily forested areas of the country. This portion is no longer connected to the original 1927 Canada-to-Florida highway, which has fallen into disuse over time, but other Florida portions of the Black Bear Trail have been preserved as part of the Florida Black Bear Scenic Highway, near Ocala about eighty miles north of Maitland.

Shouting distance from the Lake Lily Drive marker is the residence and carpentry shop of William H. Waterhouse, a pioneer who brought his wife and children from their home in New York in 1884 to reside on the quiet shore of Lake Lily. Though at one time billed as a historic museum, the modest Victorian home and carpentry shop were not offering tours as of this writing.

34
CITY OF (WINTER) HOMES

Winter Park is one of several scenic lake towns clustering around the Orlando metropolitan area, all founded around the turn of the last century. Each of them was settled by Northerners seeking a winter residence to restore the mind, body, and spirit through the winter months. The names of these towns revolve around an obvious theme: Winter Park (incorporated in 1885), Winter Haven (1911), Winter Garden (1908), Winter Springs (incorporated in 1972 but settled 1865), Frostproof (1921), and Christmas (unincorporated).

The lakes in Winter Park are famously connected by a series of quaint canals, dug by hand by the same lumberjacks who felled the pine trees used to construct the earliest homes on this lake. Scenic Boat Tours, departing from Lake Osceola, has been in continuous operation since 1933, taking visitors on slow rides through Lake Virginia, Lake Maitland, and Lake Osceola via canal. The exceptional residences of this City of Homes are often best (or only) viewed from the vantage point of their lakesides (giving a whole new meaning to the term *lakeview*).

The nickname "City of Homes" celebrates Winter Park's prodigious variety of unique residences. The abundance of tranquil lakefront homesites drew Northerners who craved Florida's balmy climate but eschewed swampland and alligators. These Central Florida lakes are expansive, blue, and tranquil, unlike the swampy Everglades or the tannic waters of the often dark and mysterious Suwannee River or the silent awfulness of Lake Okeechobee. Lake Osceola is shaped somewhat like

Lakes Virginia, Osceola, and Maitland are connected by a series of quaint canals, hand dug by the original builders of the grand homes on their banks. Originally used to transport logs for building material, today the canals accommodate scenic boat tours of the city of Homes. *Author photo.*

a butterfly, with its larger northern "wing" connecting to the immense Lake Maitland, former site of Fort Maitland. Its lower lobe or wing is connected by canal to Lake Virginia, overlooked by the scenic campus of Rollins College.

Foremost on the roster, Casa Feliz is a Spanish-style farmhouse commissioned by Massachusetts industrialist Robert Bruce Barbour in 1932. Architectural historians consider Barbour's winter residence *the* premier historic home in the City of Homes, a distinction of some note. Casa Feliz was originally constructed on Lake Osceola, at the point where its twin lobes meet on the northwest shore. Sadly, it was purchased in 2000, and the buyer planned to raze Barbour's original residence to build something more modern (and no doubt less attractive). The City of Winter Park and a group of local supporters, now known as the Friends of Casa Feliz, raised $1.2 million to move the Andalusian stone mansion across the street to the Winter Park Country Club golf course off Knowles Road. The "Happy House" is now an event venue but offers free tours.

Another nearby structure, located off Swoope Avenue, was designed by the same architect and is sometimes confused with Casa Feliz. Adding to the confusion, it has a hanging sign that reads "Barbour House." The structure is a private residence but is easily seen from the road, and any historic home tour of Winter Park would welcome its addition to the route.

Circling Lake Osceola counterclockwise, off Interlachen (German for "connecting lakes"—how apropos) is the picturesque All Saints Episcopal Church, an example of Late Gothic Revival architecture. The church was founded in 1884, and in 1941 the congregation decided to build a new church rather than repair the existing building, which was in poor shape. Note the stained-glass windows, especially the image of St. Francis of Assisi behind the altar.

Past the picturesque Women's Club of Winter Park, Interlachen bisects Fairbanks Avenue at the gateway to Rollins College. Rollins College, overlooking Lake Virginia, was founded by the Congregational Church in 1885 and maintains a beautiful campus with a number of original buildings, most notably Knowles Memorial Chapel. The dining hall overlooking Lake Virginia is open to the public, and those wishing to forgo the expensive eateries in the Winter Park downtown historic district are

An iron archway greets pedestrians passing on Osceola Avenue. Rollins College, founded in 1885 by New England Congregationalists, is home to a heavily wooded campus and classic Spanish-Mediterranean architecture; it's often named Florida's most beautiful college campus. *Author photo.*

Winter Park's Gary-Morgan House (1922) on Lake Virginia shares a shore with scenic Rollins College, Rogers's alma mater. *Author photo.*

welcome to grab a tray and an affordable lunch at the dining hall (closed during the summer months).

Continuing counterclockwise along the lower lobe of Lake Osceola is the Albin Polasek House and Studio on the lakeside of Osceola Avenue. The dwelling is set far back from the public road, but look for a bronze statue known as simply *Mother* on the sidewalk beneath the large tree. A sculptor and woodcarver from Moravia, Albin Polasek purchased three acres on Lake Osceola, where he lived from 1950 until his death in 1965. His estate consisted of his residence, a studio, sculpture gardens, a chapel (Polasek was a devout Catholic), and the historic Fern Canal connecting the lower lobe of Lake Osceola with Lake Virginia. One of Polasek's most famous sculptures is *Man Carving His Own Destiny*, which depicts a man with a chisel and hammer sculpting himself out of a block of granite. This piece can be found in the sculpture garden of Polasek's estate and is available for viewing as part of the museum walking tour.

At the corner of Osceola and Cortland Avenues is the Gary-Morgan House (1922). This Neoclassical Revival home was recently enrolled on the National Register of Historic Places; it is now a private residence overlooking Lake Virginia.

On the eastern bank of Lake Osceola, off Bonita Avenue, sits the Comstock-Harris House, or Eastbank, built in 1878 by a Chicago businessman by the name of William Comstock; it is the oldest house in Winter Park.[98] Comstock, a native of Chicago, arrived at Lake Osceola in 1877 to recover from a lengthy illness. After making a full recovery, he returned to Chicago in 1878, a strong advocate of wintering in Florida for health reasons.

Comstock initially constructed a small cottage on his sixty-acre tract. The cottage was relegated to servants' quarters in 1883 when he completed the Queen Anne mansion. A contemporary observed the mansion is much larger than it appears, with five bedrooms (each with an en suite bathroom), six fireplaces, and three pantries. The cottage and main house share a red-brick foundation. Original outbuildings included two boathouses, a barn, a caretaker's cottage, a laundry house, and a carriage house.

An 1883 description of the Comstock estate illustrates the atmosphere of Eastbank in the early days of Winter Park:

> *A short crossroad brings us to the elegant homeplace of Mr. Comstock.... Upon this place, Mr. Comstock has built a large and beautiful house, a large stable and other minor buildings, and the whole place is planted in fruit and ornamental trees, shrubs, flowers and lawns, which, with a few years' growth, will make one of the finest places in the state.*[99]

Comstock's sixty-acre tract was subdivided into smaller parcels and is today Comstock Estates. The trees Comstock planted lining the driveway leading up to his house are now the canopy trees overhanging Bonita Drive, which was once Comstock's private drive. In 1928, the Comstocks sold the property to one Mr. Harris, reduced to only three acres, for only $12,000. The Comstock-Harris estate remains in the Harris family to this day.

35

ZORA NEALE HURSTON'S CHILDHOOD HOME

Just beyond the railroad crossing of Lake Avenue, a kind of spur road connecting Orlando Avenue/FL-17 and Interstate 4, Lake becomes Kennedy Boulevard. On the right is the Kennedy Boulevard and Sewell's Place Marker, the boundary of Eatonville and Maitland, and here begins our brief detour into the childhood home of celebrated Black author and historian Zora Neale Hurston.

Eatonville, founded in 1887, was founded entirely by formerly enslaved African Americans. It is the oldest incorporated settlement to claim that distinction. In her memoir, Hurston wrote,

> *I was born in a Negro town. I do not mean by that the black, back-side of an average town. Eatonville, Florida, is, and was at the time of my birth, a pure Negro town—charter, mayor, council, town marshal and all. It was not the first Negro community in America, but it was the first to be incorporated, the first attempt at organized self-government on the part of Negroes in America.*[100]

Author of *Their Eyes Were Watching God*, Hurston was born in Alabama, but she thought of Eatonville as her home. Many of her books were set in real or fictional communities that looked a lot like Eatonville. In her fascinating essay "Eatonville, When You Look at It," she speaks of this very corner:

> *Maitland is Maitland until it gets to Hurst's corner, and then it is Eatonville. Right in front of Willie Sewell's yellow-painted house, the hard road quits being hard for a generous mile and becomes the heart of Eatonville. Or from a stranger's point of view, you could say the road just burst through on its way from Highway 17 to 441, scattering Eatonville right and left.*[101]

Hurston refers to Eatonville's boundary at US-441 in the above passage, but Interstate 4, constructed in 1965, now bisects Eatonville, slicing it right down the center in a way that feels almost cruel. The role of Interstate 4 in shaping the future of the historically Black town calls to mind its role in shaping—or crippling—the Latin Quarter in Ybor City in Tampa. Indeed, all attempts at preserving Eatonville's past abruptly end at Interstate 4, although the city's boundaries extend another one and a half miles to County Road 434. (US-441 lies just beyond.)

Another block west on Kennedy Boulevard from the Kennedy Boulevard and Sewall's Place Marker is The Mosley House Museum and St. Lawrence African Methodist Church. The Mosley House is a pre-1900 wood-frame structure typical of Eatonville and is also the home of Eatonville's first family, including Matilda Mosley, or "Tilly" as she is known in Hurston's writings. Tilly and Hurston were friends throughout their childhoods, and Hurston is said to have visited the Mosely home each time she returned to Eatonville for a visit.

Eatonville, the nation's first incorporated municipality founded entirely by former slaves, was also the childhood home of novelist, anthropologist, and historian Zora Neale Hurston, pictured here in 1938. *State Archives of Florida.*

Farther on Kennedy Boulevard another few blocks is the Eatonville Branch Library, also the site of the former Hungerford School, founded in 1889, and modeled after Booker T. Washington's Tuskegee School in Alabama. Its purpose was to provide education and moral and vocational training to boarding students from around Florida, Georgia, South Carolina, and Alabama. The Hungerford School declined after 1950 but was taken over by the public school system after integration in the 1960s and is now known as the Wymore Career Education Center.

The fast-moving Interstate 4 looms ahead as this brief snapshot of the "town that freedom built" comes to an end. A handsome Eatonville Gateway arch over Kennedy Boulevard commemorates the achievements of these hardworking early Floridians, who often had—and needed—nothing except their faith, their family, and their community. A final quote from Hurston's novel *Their Eyes Were Watching God* offers additional insight into Kennedy Boulevard in the early 1900s, after the work was over, "when the sun and the boss-man were gone" and "porch-sittin'" time began. In this part of the novel, the heroine Janie returns to Eatonville from the Everglades, where her husband, Johnny Cake, had recently died: "The people all saw her come because it was sundown. The sun was gone, but he had left his footprints in the sky. It was the time for sitting on porches beside the road. It was the time to hear things and talk."[102]

In 1960, Hurston died alone and in poverty in Fort Pierce, Florida, after suffering a stroke. The love and gratitude with which her twenty-first-century admirers have traced and preserved her contributions to Florida, evident in these monuments and preserved sites, testify to the permanence of her legacy as one of our great early Floridians.

36

MR. BOK'S BELL TOWER

Widely heralded as one of the most effective American influencers,[103] Edward William Bok wasn't even born in the United States. He moved to Brooklyn from the Netherlands at the age of six, after his well-to-do father lost his fortune through a misjudged investment decision. Bok lived in utter poverty throughout his youth, scouring the street gutters for stray bits of coal to heat his family's tenement apartment. At the age of fourteen, he quit school to take a full-time job at Western Union Telegraph Company and later worked as a stenographer at Henry Holt and Company. He was offered a position as an editor of *Brooklyn Magazine* and started his own newspaper at the age of twenty-three.

Dale Carnegie described Bok in the following way:

> *Years ago, a poor Dutch boy came to America named Edward Bok. He only went to school for six years, but he gradually became a successful magazine editor. He did so by writing to famous people and asking for information about their childhoods. He corresponded with people like James A. Garfield, Ralph Waldo Emerson, and Louisa May Alcott. Eventually he visited them at home, giving him confidence in interviewing and sparking his ambition—all because he was genuinely interested in them and wanted to listen.*[104]

Bok joined the editorial board of *Ladies' Home Journal* and ended up marrying his predecessor's daughter, Mary Louise Curtis. Under his stewardship, the publication reached a circulation of over one million subscribers, the first in the world to do so. A prolific writer as well as an editor, he published such titles as *The Americanization of Edward Bok*, *You: A Personal Message*, *Why I Believe in Poverty*, and *Successward.* An ardent antisuffragist, he swayed the opinions of millions of American women against the right to vote. He ended the advertising of patent medicines (cure-all tonics and lineaments with low effectiveness and high profits) in his publication and was faulted for publishing blueprints within reach of the average middle-class American family. He, for example, published building plans for a new architectural style out of Pasadena, California, the *bungalow*, which allowed Americans to achieve the dream of architecturally attractive homeownership for $5,000 to $8,000.

A Gothic Revival structure picturesquely situated amid a bird sanctuary and garden on Lake Wales's central ridge, Edward Bok's sixty-bell carillon tower (1926) overlooks a bucolic pond. Bok, a great admirer of balance and simplicity, planned the structure so that the pond reflects the tower's full height. *"Bok Tower Gardens" by Miles217 CC BY-SA 4.0.*

Architects accused him of cheapening their work in providing such plans at little or no cost.

Bok was widely credited with a shift in nomenclature from "parlor" or "drawing room" to "living room," and he openly criticized the gaudy, the opulent, the gilded, and the tawdry in the American family's home sphere. "We have what is called a 'drawing room,'" he famously wrote. "Just whom or what it 'draws' I have never been able to see unless it draws attention to too much money and no taste." He often wrote of what he called Christian simplicity, which he saw as rooted in the absence of Victorian clutter and excessive ornamentation. For Bok, architecture deeply affected happiness and could make or break a home, a town, and a nation. Accordingly, he was a proponent of the Arts and Crafts movement and published Frank Lloyd Wright's plans and ideas as often as he had opportunity. Wright's "architecture for every man," which came to be known as Prairie style, disposed of a domineering box-shaped structure in favor of low, horizontal lines and open interior spaces, mimicking the openness and domesticity of the American prairie. In this way, Wright wrote, the family home would be a community, blurring the lines between recreation and work, indoors and outdoors, the private and the open space.

In 1921, Edward and Mary Bok visited Central Florida on the Lake Wales Ridge.[105] Bok was immediately drawn to the prolific flora and fauna of Central Florida and felt compelled to protect the land from development. He purchased twenty-five acres, which he immediately set about transforming into a bird sanctuary. He imported one thousand live oaks, ten thousand azaleas, one hundred sabal palms, three hundred magnolias, five hundred gardenias, and myriad fruit bushes such as blueberry and holly. The Boks introduced a splendid variety of fauna, though some species fared better than others. The flamingo wasn't cold hardy enough to survive the Central Florida winters, being native to South Florida, and was also preyed on by other wildlife; nightingales imported from England also lacked the tolerance to cold requisite for Lake Wales winters.

In 1925, he installed the 205-foot stone tower that has now assumed his name. Bok Tower is a Gothic Revival structure essentially purposed to house a sixty-bell carillon, a bell instrument made of cast bronze bells that remain stationary and are struck with wooden clappers, controlled by a keyboard below. The carillon was first developed in sixteenth-century Belgium and the Netherlands. Faithful to Bok's core principles of simplicity and absence of waste, his tower accomplished more than lilting melody. The first floor served as Bok's personal study; the third housed a water reservoir; its fifth contained a library of carillon music said to be the largest in the world; the sixth held the keyboard controlling the clappers; and the seventh served as a workroom.

Bok died in 1930, just nine years after discovering his Lake Wales retreat and just five years following the completion of his tower. His departure was a relatively peaceful one: he suffered a heart attack at Valentino, his private residence in nearby Mountain Lake Estates, in view of his beloved Bell Tower.

Bok is buried at the base of his tower; he gifted his garden to the people of the United States in thankfulness, he said, to all they had done for him in his lifetime. Today, Bok Tower is a 250-acre contemplative garden, including the tower with the sixty-bell carillon. The grounds also include Bok Exedra, a semicircular bench dedicated to Bok's memory by his neighbors in Mountain Lake Estates and made of the same rose and gray marble as Bok Tower. Also on campus and available for tours is El Retiro, a twenty-room Mediterranean mansion adjacent to Bok's original gardens acquired by his descendants in the 1970s to enhance the beauty of the garden.

TREASURE COAST

37
MINORCAN SETTLEMENT OF NEW SMYRNA

The Spanish ceded La Florida to England in 1763, opening for colonization huge swaths of East Florida to British settlement. In its program to populate its newly acquired land, Great Britain arranged huge land grants with English nobility with the condition they introduce settlers to the land.

The British Crown selected Dr. Andrew Turnbull of Scotland as the recipient of one of these grants, requiring him to settle the area at a ratio of one person for every one hundred acres.

Dr. Turnbull set about immediately fulfilling his end of the agreement, but he recognized that his compatriots in misty Scotland and Ireland would fail to thrive in Florida's subtropical terrain. Another Englishman, Denys Rolles had attempted to emulate James Oglethorpe's successful debtors' colony in Georgia by bringing prisoners, criminals, and other undesirables to work and live near modern-day Palatka. Yet Rolles's colony failed because the Englishmen he recruited fared poorly in the heat and humidity of the Florida frontier. Instead of Englishmen, Dr. Turnbull recruited Mediterranean natives for his colony. Olive-skinned with shining black hair and flashing eyes, his recruits came from Italy, Greece, and Spain and were accustomed to salt and intense sunshine.

Having made his plan, Turnbull visited the Mediterranean countries seeking recruits, but government officials did not wish to see their subjects leave for an unknown land with a Protestant Scotchman. Most of the Mediterranean lands were still Roman Catholic and did not take kindly to

Scottish physician Lord Andrew Turnbull arrived in the then-British colony of East Florida in 1768, along with 1,300 Minorcan indentured servants and the supplies for a new startup colony. His venture lasted only nine short years, as clashes with Native Americans, a harsh environment, and gross mismanagement plagued his colony from its inception. *State Archives of Florida.*

releasing their subjects—even the poorest of the poor or those living outside the law. Turnbull met with the most success in the Spanish island of Minorca, rounding up 1,300 citizens; he promised the workers fifty acres of land after three years of indentured servitude. By and large, Turnbull reneged on the contracts.

Agriculture was the industry of choice in La Florida, and indigo, cotton, and sugar were all viable cash crops for a new British colony. Turnbull arrived in 1768 on a ship with a solid plan and 1,300 workers, plus the necessary items to start a new town. He picked the name Smyrna for his colony, after his Greek wife's native island.

Several factors contributed to the almost immediate failure of Turnbull's design. First, his recruits, though more accustomed to sweltering temperatures than their Anglo-Saxon counterparts, still struggled in the Florida wilderness. Malaria, stifling heat and humidity, and the constant threat of Seminole raids disrupted life in New Smyrna. Second, the religious differences between colonial leadership and the indentured populace strained governance: The Minorcans were Roman Catholic, while Turnbull and his colleagues were Protestant. Each side doubted the good character of the other, making teamwork impossible. Finally, Turnbull was a poor businessman and showed little financial judgment, leading to sluggish financial growth, delayed or nonexistent fulfillment of indentured servitude contracts, and a disgruntled and strained workforce.

In 1777, a group of protesting Minorcan colonists marched to St. Augustine to seek asylum with the British governor, complaining of ill treatment and inhumane conditions in New Smyrna. St. Photios Greek Orthodox National Shrine in St. Augustine was founded in 1985 by the descendants of these transplanted New Smyrna colonists.

Later, Spain took Florida back from England, and Turnbull escaped his failed project by moving to Charleston, South Carolina. Those remaining colonists who hadn't died from poor conditions or already sought refuge in St. Augustine in 1777 left New Smyrna to join the original group in St. Augustine. Now back in the hands of Catholic Spain, the flourishing Catholic city offered the Minorcan nationals plenty of opportunity to thrive. Many of the descendants of this remnant continue to populate St. Augustine today.

The site of the colony remained vacant for a century after its abandonment by Turnbull and the Minorcans. Florida became an American colony in 1821 and then a state in 1845, but New Smyrna remained isolated and unpopular due to Seminole conflicts and its standing reputation as a poor site for settlement. Moreover, the Ponce de Leon Inlet was at that time called Mosquito Inlet (it wouldn't be renamed Ponce de Leon Inlet until 1922). This, coupled with the failure of Turnbull's town, caused newcomers to select other locales. By the time it was incorporated in 1887, New Smyrna had a population of only 150. Soon after New Smyrna's incorporation, Henry Flagler's wildly popular East Coast Railway added the town as a whistlestop, attracting more Northerners by the beginning of the twentieth century. During 1920s Prohibition, New Smyrna's proximity to the Caribbean and the railway made it a hub of bootleggers and rumrunners, adding indirectly to a blossoming local (lawful) economy.

Although Turnbull and his colonists abandoned the project after nine short years, ample reminders of the New Smyrna colony remain on site. Its name, of course, dates to the failed settlement; the city of New Smyrna was incorporated in 1887. (It became New Smyrna Beach in 1947 with the city's acquisition of nearby Coronado Beach.)

Moreover, New Smyrna Beach's canal system originated with Dr. Turnbull. He carefully studied the Egyptian system of irrigation and attempted to emulate it in New Smyrna. During the colony's nine years of existence, colonists and Black slaves dug three east–west canals for drainage of its indigo, rice, and hemp fields, connected by one perpendicular Grand Canal that ran north–south. These waterways dug by colonists in the 1760s are still visible in New Smyrna's trendy Canal Street District and are remembered in business and public titles, such as Canal Street and The Hub on the Canal.

New Smyrna Beach's tabby ruins located near the Canal Historic District are perhaps the most intriguing of the colonial monuments.[106] Old Fort Park, one block north of the canal, has drawn local fascination for more than two hundred years. Though labeled colloquially as "Old Fort" (also the name of the public park), the origin of the ruins is still a

The earliest maps and long-standing local custom call these mysterious stone ruins "Turnbull's Fort," but the truth is their origin is unknown. A Spanish mission, the ghost of a vanished pre-Turnbull settlement, storage structures related to Turnbull's failed Minorcan colony, or the unfinished residence of Lord Turnbull himself have all been proposed. *"Turnbull Ruins, New Smyrna Beach" by Che-or CC BY-SA 4.0.*

mystery. An 1817 map labeled the site Turnbull's Palace, and thereafter, maps and official documents name it alternatively Turnbull castle, the Turnbull mansion or the Turnbull fort. Yet it is dubious that Turnbull constructed a stone castle according to some archaeologists, who claim that the walls aren't thick enough to serve as a fortress. Others suggest as possible explanations a Spanish mission called San Pedro shown on some early maps, or infrastructure related to the production of indigo. Adding to the intrigue of the site, it was discovered in the late 1990s that the stone ruins are situated on an ancient Indian burial mound. This discovery both enhanced the mystery and precluded its solution: The site being designated a "sacred ground" curtails the possibility of some efforts at further investigation or fieldwork. (This dichotomy of the different aims of historical preservation—protecting Indian burial grounds as well as subsequent European development—echoes the holding pattern at the

Jungle Prada site in St. Petersburg.) Most viable today is the hypothesis that the stone ruins are Turnbull's incomplete personal residence, which some evidence suggests was under construction in 1778 when Turnbull vacated the site.

Whatever their origin, the ruins are open and public today at Old Fort Park on the shore of the Indian River, at the disposal for exploring and conjecturing of the next generation of New Smyrnaeans and curious outsiders.

38
PONCE DE LEON INLET LIGHTHOUSE

Mosquito Inlet was its former name—not exactly a welcoming title. Its position on the wild Atlantic Ocean, with no gulf, bay, or harbor to offer protection, made the east coast of Florida relatively empty through most of history. Bookended by major metropolitan areas in the north (Jacksonville) and the south (Fort Lauderdale and Miami), the two-hundred-mile stretch of Florida from St. Augustine to West Palm Beach lacks major population centers. NASA and Kennedy Space Center elevated the status of this area after the 1960s; other development has been sluggish or nonexistent. Mosquito Inlet was renamed Ponce de Leon Inlet in 1922 in direct response to the former appellation's repelling effect.

Back in the 1830s, this stretch of coastline was all but desolate. The occasional skirmish with Seminole tribes erupted, but for the most part Turnbull's "Old Fort" ruins spent many decades alone with the sand dunes and the sea spray. However, the Indian River and the Halifax River empty into the Atlantic Ocean at this point, and plantation owners made rather consistent use of the inlet to export citrus and sugar. In 1830, William DePeyster of the Crugar-DePeyster Sugar Mill ruins near New Smyrna Beach petitioned Congress to build a lighthouse to assist in the transportation of his sugar, hemp, and rum. In 1834, Congress responded by building a white, cone-shaped brick tower on the south side of the channel and allocating an annual stipend of $450 (though it failed to supply its first lighthouse keeper with oil to light the lamp, so he had little to do that first year).[107] In October 1835, the lighthouse keeper's quarters were washed into the Atlantic Ocean in an especially violent late-season storm. Thereafter, frequent attacks by Seminoles plagued the lighthouse. In one such incident, a Seminole chief broke into the tower itself and climbed the stairwell, retrieving the reflectors, fashioning a warrior's headdress from the shiny material.

In 1836, that first tower totally collapsed, and the Ponce de Leon Inlet went dark for several decades. Clashes with Seminole tribes and the onslaught of the Civil War precluded a new light project, though the Lighthouse Board acknowledged the need. Ponce de Leon Inlet is approximately halfway between two other major lighthouses, St. Augustine and Cape Canaveral, and no other navigational aid existed on this one-hundred-mile stretch.

The inlet remained in the dark until 1884, when at last the Lighthouse Board responded by sending crews to begin clearing brush and leveling the ground for a lighthouse on its north side, the south side having proved unstable due to the flow of the current. Ironically, a lighthouse official sustained a fatal shipwreck at the inlet on his way to survey the construction work for the new tower.

The tallest lighthouse in Florida (and the second tallest in the United States) greets motorists along famed US-1, its iconic fire engine–red daymark dominating the western aspect of Ponce de Leon Inlet. Only Cape Hatteras Lighthouse off North Carolina is taller. *"Ponce de Leon Inlet Lighthouse" by PA Uploader CCO.*

On November 1, 1887, the second tower finally ignited its light for the first time. One million bricks were used in the construction of the 175-foot tower. The Ponce de Leon Inlet Lighthouse is the second tallest in the United States, behind only Cape Hatteras in North Carolina (known as the Graveyard of the Atlantic due to the number of fatal ships historically wrecked on its shoals). Its foundation extends twelve feet into the sand, providing lasting stability.

Toward the end of the nineteenth century, *Red Badge of Courage* author Stephen Crane was sailing to Cuba for a firsthand investigation into the Cuban struggle for independence from Spain. En route, his vessel crashed near present-day Daytona.

Crane and three other men spent twenty-seven hours frantically rowing and fighting the waves and were saved only by the distant beacon of the Ponce de Leon Inlet Lighthouse, ten miles south of the site of the wreck. Crane famously wrote of this experience in his short story "Open Boat."

> *"See it?" said the captain.*
>
> *"No," said the correspondent, slowly, "I didn't see anything."*
>
> *"Look again," said the captain. He pointed. "It's exactly in that direction." At the top of another wave, the correspondent did as he was bid, and this time his eyes chanced on a small still thing on the edge of the swaying horizon. It was precisely like the point of a pin. It took an anxious eye to find a lighthouse so tiny.*[108]

39

GILBERT'S BAR AND *GEORGES VALENTINE* SHIPWRECK

Between 1876 and 1886, ten lifesaving stations were installed along Florida's treacherous east coast, susceptible to shipwreck especially because of an absence of a protective gulf and few harbors or bays. Prior to the stations' construction, mariners knew Florida's east coast to be a "howling wilderness" with no people, food, or water for miles of totally empty and remote shoreline.[109] A major shipwreck near present-day Fort Lauderdale in 1873 caught the attention of the federal government, in which surviving sailors were found days later surviving on bad fish and brackish water. Their attempts to flag down passing ships were ignored or missed, and by the time they were finally rescued they were half-starved and nearly dead. Following this incident, five houses of refuge were constructed along Florida's east coast: Vero Beach, Stuart, Delray Beach, Fort Lauderdale, and Miami Beach. At this time, these locations were sparsely populated or had not yet come into existence.

House of Refuge No. 1 was at Fort Pierce Inet, and the site is now a city park.

House of Refuge No. 2 was called Gilbert's Bar House of Refuge (1876) and is the oldest structure in Martin County today. Although *bar* may conjure up an image of an innocent sandbar, Gilbert's Bar refers to a two-mile stretch of treacherous, jagged rocks along the coastline. Gilbert's Bar is also known as the St. Lucie Rocks and is part of the Anastasia Formation, a rocky ridge that spans the east coast of Florida from St. Augustine to Miami. The name *Anastasia* comes from its northern reaches on Anastasia

Island near St. Augustine. The Spanish quarried a portion of the geological formation for the construction of the Castillo de San Marcos in the late 1600s to protect the tiny Spanish colony from Native Americans, roaming pirates, and the English.

Gilbert's Bar is the only House of Refuge extant of the original ten and was saved by the Martin County Historical Society in 1955. One reason for its preservation may be the underwater archeological preserve that sits just offshore from the House. In 1905, *Georges Valentine*, an Italian ship, crashed on the rocks, and seven of its twelve crew survived the wreck. The first man ashore was Viktor Erikson of Sweden carrying a fellow crewmate on his back. The men somehow reached the House of Refuge, despite the deadly shoal separating them from safety.

Viktor awoke the keeper on duty, Captain William E. Rea, who immediately entered the stormy seas to attempt to recover the other crewmen. Viktor Erikson sat on a high rock with a lantern to assist any survivors with reaching the safety of the shore and to keep an eye on Captain Rea.

The sole remaining structure of the original ten, Gilbert's Bar House of Refuge (1876) boasts a colorful and intriguing history, including the demise of Italian ship *Georges Valentine* in 1905. *State Archives.*

Captain Rea was able to rescue five other crewmen, placing the total survivor county at seven. The other five crewmen had *Georges Valentine* as their grave. In the same storm, another ship ran aground on the Gilbert's Bar, and Captain Rea and his wife assisted the crew in its recovery along with the crew of *Georges Valentine*. A few weeks later, Captain Rea was able to transport the men, a total of twenty-two between the two crews. Typical of the period, the crews of both international vessels consisted of men from many different nations. All crewmen returned home except for one Edward Sarkenglov, who changed his name to "Big Ed" and became a local fisherman.

Later Captain Rea said of the experience,

> *In these two crews we had a Scotch, Russian, Italian, Spanish and Swedish, and they were all as nice a lot of men that ever came ashore. When I finally got them off to Jacksonville the men stood up and the captain* [of Georges Valentine] *put his arms around me and said, "Master, Good-bye! We no more see you."*[110]

Today, *Georges Valentine* is an underwater archaeological preserve, one of eleven in the state of Florida. Both Gilbert's Bar House of Refuge and *Georges Valentine* are listed on the National Register of Historic Places.

40

JUPITER INLET LIGHTHOUSE

Route US-1, the famous road stretching from the dusty, packed streets of Old Key West to the misty reaches of the Maine hinterland, passes a colorful lighthouse north of Palm Beach, the final detour for Central Florida. Its red daymark rises handsomely in the distance as US-1 crosses the Loxahatchee River from island to mainland.

Though plans were laid for construction of a red lighthouse on a small hill at Jupiter Inlet in 1853, the Third Seminole War broke out in 1855, pausing plans due to open conflict between the United States and local Seminoles.[111] The lighthouse was finally completed in 1860, just prior to President Abraham Lincoln signing the Emancipation Proclamation, the start of the War Between the States.

Shortly after the commencement of the Civil War, three unidentified men entered the lighthouse grounds and stole the "illuminating apparatus," though they destroyed nothing and left all other parts intact. They wrote a letter to Governor Perry informing him of their deed but assured him the parts in question were under lock and key and would be returned at the close of the war. (The missing parts were later discovered in palmetto bushes near Lake Worth Creek.) Removing or disabling navigational beacons on Florida's coast was a common practice during the Civil War. This often set up an uncomfortable and tenuous relationship between lighthouse keeper, locals (almost always Confederate), and the Lighthouse Board (usually Unionist). Depending on the allegiances of the lighthouse keeper and his assistant, complicity, blissful ignorance, apathy, reluctant acceptance, attempted resistance, or all-out violent defense characterized the response of the keeper to attempts to disable his light.

The post as lighthouse keeper at the utterly remote Jupiter Inlet was often a lonely one: in 1867, Keeper Armour brought his new wife, Almeda Carlile, to his new post, where she would be the only non-Native woman for over one hundred miles. The couple remained at the lighthouse for more than forty years, faithfully illuminating the safety of the inlet for passing mariners every evening with no break. The Armours had eight children. At first, they were homeschooled, but then they began to attend a one-room schoolhouse up the Loxahatchee River. They and other frontier children living on the Loxahatchee River boarded a crude boat each morning to get to school, which was known as the Octagon School because of its shape.

Their sack lunches often contained bear meat sandwiches, as the older Armour boys hunted the occasional bear that wandered into the inlet to prey on turtle eggs. This would have supplemented the family's meals, which consisted of fish, occasional meat from other game, kitchen garden vegetables, and dry goods from the meager salary the lighthouse keeper was allotted by the Lighthouse Board.

When Keeper Armour finally retired in 1908, his son-in-law took over his post for him. A few of the Armour grandchildren are buried in the small graveyard near the historic keeper's quarters at Jupiter Inlet.

By 1928, the light had been converted to electric power, but lighthouse keeper Captain Seabrook and his son learned that sometimes the old-fashioned ways are better. That summer, a huge hurricane knocked out the power to the lighthouse, extinguishing the light and rendering the inlet dark. Captain Seabrook installed the recently retired oil lamp, but the iron-ball rotation system had been disabled several months before due to the conversion to electric power. At this time, Captain Seabrook was fighting a severe infection in his hand, but faithful to his post, he commenced manually rotating the lamp despite his pain.

Seabrook's sixteen-year-old son, Franklin, noticing his father's infection, volunteered to rotate the lamp to keep the navigational aid functioning until dawn. As he climbed the steps to enter the tower, he was blown back four times by the powerful hurricane-force wind. He manually rotated the flame, keeping as regular a timing as possible, for four full hours before he was relieved. During this time, he later wrote, he could hear the mortar cracking between the bricks as the iron bars suspending the lantern room above the stone tower were giving out. The glass of the lantern room was shattered during the storm, and the lens broke, but the light did not go out. (The damage sustained by the lens is visible in an enormous X on the bull's-eye lens despite subsequent repairs.)

Later in 1931, that same Captain Seabrook planted the immense banyan tree that graces the Jupiter Inlet Lighthouse Museum and Park property to this day.

NOTES

WEST-CENTRAL

1. Michael D'Orso, *Like Judgment Day: The Ruin and Redemption of a Town Called Rosewood* (Boulevard Books, 1996).
2. National Register of Historic Places, Eugene Knotts House, Yankeetown, Levy County, Florida, National Register #100002066.
3. National Register of Historic Places, Eugene Knotts House.
4. National Register of Historic Places, Dade Battlefield Memorial State Park, Bushnell, Sumter County, Florida, National Register #72000353.
5. "Pilaklikaha / Abraham's Town Historical Marker," Historical Marker Database, https://www.hmdb.org.
6. National Register of Historic Places, Howey Mansion, Howey-in-the-Hills, Lake County, Florida, National Register #83001426.
7. National Register of Historic Places, Chinsegut Hill Manor House, Brooksville, Hernando County, Florida, National Register #03001171.
8. George M. Barbour, *Florida for Tourists, Invalids and Settlers* (University of Florida Press, 1964), 58.
9. *De Soto Trail: De Soto National Historic Trail Study (National Park Service Southeast Regional Office,* 1990), 13–14, *https://npshistory.com.*
10. Richard J. Stanaback, *A History of Hernando County* (Daniels Publishers, 1976), 24–25.
11. Stanaback, *History of Hernando County*, 119–20.
12. Stanaback, *History of Hernando County*, 119–20.

13. Gregg Turner, *A Short History of Florida Railroads* (Arcadia Publishing, 2003), 59–60.
14. James J. Horgan, *Pioneer College: The Centennial History of Saint Leo College, Saint Leo Abbey, and Holy Names Priory* (Saint Leo College Press, 1989), 25.
15. Horgan, *Pioneer College*, 478.
16. Horgan, *Pioneer College*, 419.

TAMPA METRO AREA

17. R.F. Pent, *History of Tarpon Springs* (Great Outdoors Publishing Company, 1964).
18. Amy F. David, "Odet Philippe: Peninsula Pioneer," *Sunland Tribune* 24, article 9 (1998).
19. "History of the Jungle Prado Building (Now Called Jungle Prada)," *The Jungle Country Club History Project*, https://junglecountryclubhistoryproject.blogspot.com.
20. Cynthia Williams, "The Don CeSar: Florida's Grand Hotel Has an Intriguing History," Historic Hotels of America, In the News, https://www.historichotels.org.
21. "The Don Ce-Sar: A Castle Made of Sand," St. Pete Wiki, https://stpetewiki.com.
22. "Our History in St. Petersburg," The Don CeSar, https://www.doncesar.com.
23. "Egmont Key Lighthouse," Lighthouse Friends, https://www.lighthousefriends.com.
24. John F. Hagan to *Tallahassee Sentinel*, February 1852, in "Egmont Key Lighthouse."
25. Erika Desonie, Baron Reichenbach, Delaney Streicher, Joseph Vars, Kathleen Weibley, "Pass-a-Postcard," https://storymaps.arcgis.com.
26. Anne Field, "Biography of Zephaniah Phillips (1837–1903)," Anne's Genealogy, http://annefield.net.
27. "Pass-A-Grille: Gulf Florida's First Beach," *Florida Traveler*, May 12, 2020, https://floridatraveler.org.
28. National Register of Historic Places, Ybor City Historic District, Tampa, Hillsborough County, Florida, National Register #74000641.
29. E.J. Salcines, "Tampa: Untold Stories with E.J. Salcines-West Tampa," directed by Brian Sullivan, recorded lecture, filmed July 27, 2018, 47 minutes long, https://www.youtube.com.
30. "First Generation, Casimiro, Senior and Adela Hernandez," 1905 Family of Restaurants, https://www.1905familyofrestaurants.com.
31. "Second Generation, Casimiro, Junior and Carmen Hernandez," 1905 Family of Restaurants, https://www.1905familyofrestaurants.com.
32. Manny Leto, "Ybor City's Broadway Bakery." *Cigar City Magazine*, July/August 2007.
33. City of Tampa Code of Ordinances, Section 27-177(c) (2024).

34. Thomas Swick, "'Now You're in Cuba': Tampa's Ybor City Is the Country's Original Little Havana," *Atlanta Magazine*, April 6, 2017.
35. "Historic Tour of Downtown Ybor City, Tampa: The Latin Quarter Turns from Cigars to Entertainment," Florida History, https://www.floridahistory.org.
36. National Register of Historic Places, Hyde Park Historic Districts, Tampa, Hillsborough County, Florida, National Register #85000454.
37. Hernando Escalante de Fontaneda, *Memoir of the Things, the Shore, and the Indians of Florida, to Describe which, None of the Many Persons Who Have Coasted That Country Knows How to Describe It*, trans. Buckingham Smith (Washington, 1854).
38. Rebecca O'Sullivan, "What Does This Storm Drain Have to Do with Archeology?" *Experience Archeology*, January 2013.
39. "The Sulphur Springs Water Tower," Tampa Pix, https://tampapix.com.

Southwest Central (Bradenton to Charlotte Harbor)

40. *De Soto Trail.*
41. John D. Ware, "A View of Celi's Journal of Surveys and Chart of 1757," *Florida Historical Quarterly* 47, no. 1 (July 1968): 8–24.
42. Anna Maria Riles, *Island Homestead: Interview with Anna Maria Cobb Riles and Humbug Cobb* (Manatee County Public Library System, 1969).
43. "Anna Maria Island History," Anna Maria Island Chamber of Commerce, https://annamariaislandchamber.org.
44. Anna Maria Island Code of Ordinances, Ord. No. 16-824, Section 1, 12-8-16.
45. National Register of Historic Places, Cortez Historic District, Bradenton, Manatee County, Florida, National Register #95000250.
46. National Register of Historic Places, Cortez Historic District.
47. Samuel Curtis Upham, *Notes from Sunland, on the Manatee River, Gulfcoast of South Florida* (Claxton & Claxton, 1881), 39–45.
48. Rodney H. Kite-Powell, "The Escape of Judah P. Benjamin," *Sunland Tribune* 22, article 9 (1996).
49. Daughters of the American Revolution Sara De Soto Chapter, "Mary Wyatt Whitaker," Historical Marker, 1936, Sarasota, Florida.
50. Kite-Powell, "Escape of Judah P. Benjamin," 6.
51. Upham, *Notes from Sunland*, 45.
52. Upham, *Notes from Sunland*, 10–17.
53. Vickie Oldham, "Escaped Slave Community of Angola," Tampa/St. Petersburg, Florida: American History TV on C-SPAN3, May 12, 2011.

54. National Register of Historic Places, Braden Castle Park Historic District, Bradenton, Manatee County, Florida, National Register #83001428.
55. Upham, *Notes from Sunland*, 43.
56. National Register of Historic Places, Braden Castle Park Historic District.
57. John and Mable Ringling Museum of Art, *Cà d'Zan, Ringling Residence* (Ringling Museum, 1954), 8–9.
58. Ron McCarty, Ringling Museum of Art and Sarasota County History Center, "Mable Burton Ringling," Sarasota History Alive!, https://www.sarasotahistoryalive.com.
59. Meghan White, "What Is Italianate Architecture?" National Trust for Historic Preservation, April 16, 2019, https://savingplaces.org.
60. *Oxford English Dictionary*, 2nd ed. (Oxford University Press, 2004), s.v. "Gazebo."
61. Brion Palmer, "The Landings Iconic Banyan Trees," *Landings-Eagle Extra*, May 2023, https://issuu.com.
62. Meg Lowman, "Ringling's Living Museum—One of Nature's Best-Kept Local Secrets," *Sarasota Herald-Tribune*, February 25, 2007.
63. Hope L. Black, "Mounted on a Pedestal: Bertha Honoré Palmer" (USF Tampa Graduate Theses and Dissertations, 2007), 26–27.
64. Black, "Mounted on a Pedestal," 26–27.
65. Black, "Mounted on a Pedestal," 29.
66. Black, "Mounted on a Pedestal," 16.
67. Black, "Mounted on a Pedestal," 55–59.
68. Black, "Mounted on a Pedestal," 79.
69. Black, "Mounted on a Pedestal," 100–101.
70. Black, "Mounted on a Pedestal," 1.
71. Audio selection, "Interview with Claude Sheppard," 1958, C77-5, Florida Crackers, Folklife, Exhibits, State Archives of Florida, Tallahassee, Florida, https://floridamemory.com.
72. Charlotte Tucker, "Myakka: A Community Portrait," Sarasota County Historical Association (circa 1984).
73. Jana Futch, "Historical Archaeology of the Pine Level Site (8DE14), DeSoto County, Florida" (USF, Tampa Graduate Theses and Dissertations, 2011), https://digitalcommons.usf.edu.
74. Lindsay Williams and U.S. Cleveland, *OUR Fascinating Past Charlotte Harbor Area: The Early Years* (Charlotte Harbor Area Historical Society, 2005), 102–8.
75. Tucker, "Myakka."
76. Tucker, "Myakka."
77. Bonnie Gross, "Myakka River State Park," *Florida Rambler*, July 30, 2023, https://www.floridarambler.com.

78. Dan Wagner, "Explore Deep Hole in Florida's Myakka River State Park," Great American Hikes, https://www.greatamericanhikes.com.
79. John J. Sullivan, "Conservation Civilian Corps and the Creation of Myakka River State Park," Tampa Bay History 9, no. 2 (1987).

CENTRAL LAKES REGION

80. Marjorie Kinnan Rawlings, *Cross Creek Cookery* (Fireside, 1942), 7.
81. Rawlings, *Cross Creek Cookery*, 180.
82. Forest Service-U.S. Department of Agriculture, "Yearling Trail," National Forests in Florida, https://www.fs.usda.gov.
83. William Bartram, "Chapter VI" in *The Travels of William Bartram*, ed. Mark VanDuren (Macy-Masius, 1928), 163–64.
84. Bartram, "Chapter VI."
85. Bartram, "Chapter VI."
86. National Register of Historic Places, Micanopy Historic District, Micanopy, Alachua County, Florida, National Register #77841955.
87. Kevin McCarthy, *The History of Micanopy* (Kevin McCarthy, 2021).
88. National Register of Historic Places, Micanopy Historic District.
89. Lars Anderson, *Paynes Prairie: The Great Savanna, A History and Guide*, 2nd ed. (Pineapple Press, 2003).
90. Carl Webber, *The Eden of the South…Alachua County, Florida* (Leve & Alden, 1883), 58.
91. McCarthy, *History of Micanopy*, 83.
92. Gary McKechnie and Nancy Howell, *A Brief History of Mt. Dora, Florida* (The History Press, 2016).
93. McKechnie and Howell, *Brief History*, 43.
94. C.E. Spooner, *Narrow Gauge Railways*, 2nd ed. (William Clowes & Sons, 1879).
95. National Register of Historic Places, Longwood Hotel, Longwood, Orange County, Florida, National Register #84000963.
96. National Register of Historic Places, Longwood Hotel.
97. "Maitland's Lake Lily Was Known as John's Hole," Florida History–Orange County, April 19, 2023, https://floridahistoryblog.com.
98. National Register of Historic Places, Comstock-Harris House, Winter Park, Orange County, Florida, National Register #83001432.
99. National Register of Historic Places, Comstock-Harris House.
100. Zora N. Hurston, *Dust Tracks on a Road: A Memoir* (Lippincott, 1942).

101. Zora N. Hurston, "Eatonville, When You Look at It," in *Go Gator and Muddy the Water: Writings by Zora Neale Hurston from the Federal Writers Project,* edited by Pamela Bordelon (W.W. Norton & Co., 1999).
102. Zora N. Hurston, *Their Eyes Were Watching God* (Lippincott, 1937).
103. See, for example, Dale Carnegie's *How to Win Friends and Influence People* (Simon & Schuster, 1934).
104. Carnegie, *How to Win Friends.*
105. Edward Bok, *America's Taj Mahal* (Bok Tower Gardens Foundation, 1989).

TREASURE COAST

106. National Register of Historic Places, Old Fort Park, New Smyrna Beach, Volusia County, Florida, National Register #08000629.
107. Kraig Anderson, "Ponce de Leon Inlet Lighthouse," Lighthouse Friends, https://lighthousefriends.com.
108. Stephen Crane, "Open Boat," in *The Open Boat and Other Tales of Adventure* (Doubleday, 1898).
109. National Register of Historic Places, Gilbert's Bar House of Refuge, Stuart, Martin County, Florida, National Register of Historic #74000651.
110. Brochure, Florida Department of State, Division of Historical Resources, Bureau of Archeological Research, "*Georges Valentine* Underwater Archeological Preserve, Stuart, FL," https://museumsinthesea.com.
111. Kraig Anderson, "Jupiter Inlet Lighthouse," Lighthouse Friends, https://lighthousefriends.com.

ABOUT THE AUTHOR

Jennifer McCollum Husmann was born and raised in Central Florida. Her ancestors arrived as soon as it was opened for settlement, raising cattle and tending orange groves. Husmann attended the University of Florida in Gainesville, where she graduated with a degree in English and later earned a law degree. She met her future husband in 2007 while visiting her parents in Tampa. Jennifer and Ryan were married in Pass-A-Grille near St. Pete Beach and then lived in Land O' Lakes north of Tampa. For the last decade, Jennifer has lived with her husband and three children in rural Sarasota near Miakka.